The Seedbed Daily Text

THIS

IS HOW

WE KNOW

1 John

J. D. WALT

Seedbed

Unless otherwise indicated, Scripture quotations are taken from the Holy Bible, New International Version®, NIV® Copyright ©1973, 1978, 1984, 2011 by Biblica, Inc.® Used by permission. All rights reserved worldwide.

Scripture quotations marked ESV are taken from The Holy Bible, English Standard Version. ESV® Permanent Text Edition® (2016). Copyright © 2001 by Crossway Bibles, a publishing ministry of Good News Publishers.

Scripture quotations marked HCSB are taken from the Holman Christian Standard Bible (HCSB) Copyright © 1999, 2000, 2002, 2003, 2009 by Holman Bible Publishers, Nashville Tennessee. All rights reserved.

Scripture quotations marked KJ21 are taken from the 21st Century King James Version (KJ21) Copyright © 1994 by Deuel Enterprises, Inc.

Scripture quotations marked NASB are taken from the New American Standard Bible®, Copyright © 1960, 1962, 1963, 1968, 1971, 1972, 1973, 1975, 1977, 1995 by The Lockman Foundation Used by permission. www.Lockman.org

All italics in Scriptures in this text are the author's own emphasis.

Printed in the United States of America

Cover and page design by Strange Last Name
Page layout by PerfecType, Nashville, Tennessee

Walt, John David.
 This is how we know : 1 John / J.D. Walt. – Frankin, Tennessee : Seedbed Publishing, ©2017.

  xii, 132 pages ; 21 cm. – (The Seedbed daily text)

  ISBN 9781628244632 (paperback)
  ISBN 9781628244649 (Mobi)
  ISBN 9781628244656 (ePub)
  ISBN 9781628244663 (uPDF)

  1. Bible. Epistle of John, 1st--Devotional literature. 2. Bible. Epistle of John, 1st--Prayers and devotions. 3. Bible. Epistle of John, 1st --Meditations.   I. Title. II. Seedbed daily text.

BS2805.45.W34 2017   242/.5   2017949907

SEEDBED PUBLISHING
Franklin, Tennessee
seedbed.com

THIS

IS HOW

WE KNOW

For my children,
David, Mary Kathryn, Lily, and Samuel,
the brightest stars in my sky.

Contents

Introduction   ix

1. I Believe John   1
2. The Seduction of the Middle   2
3. The Antidote to Self-Deception   5
4. Dealing with the Biggest "If" in Life   7
5. On Preachers and Sermons versus
   Communicators and Messages   9
6. Reframing Sin   12
7. The Game-Changing Question of Easter   14
8. Love Is Not Soft; It's Hard   17
9. Love Cannot Be Taught; Only Demonstrated   20
10. Lost Is Not a Subjective Feeling;
    It's an Objective Reality   23
11. When Sin Gets Redefined as Not Sin   27
12. Why the Problem Is Not Pornography   31
13. The Greatest Danger to the Church: Then and Now   34
14. Do You Have the Anointing?   37
15. The Exclusive Inclusive Gospel of Jesus Christ   41
16. The Simple Simplicity of Abiding in the Gospel   43
17. How to Spot a Counterfeit   46
18. Why Attention Is More Important Than Activity   49
19. If Sin Has Lost Its Power, How Can It Keep
    on Winning?   53
20. Why Sinning Is Not Inevitable   55

21. The Orange Juice Concentrate Approach to Faith versus Simply Orange — 58
22. The Powerful Principle of Displacement — 61
23. "I'm a Mac, and I'm a PC": How the Great Leaders Lead Change — 64
24. Are You Saved? Are You Sure? How Do You Know? — 66
25. Why the Rest of the Gospel Is the Best of the Gospel — 69
26. People Need Help, Not Pity — 72
27. Why You Shouldn't Trust Your Conscience — 75
28. How Condemnation Works and Why It Loses — 78
29. The Difference between Certainty and Clarity — 81
30. Put Your Leaders to the Test — 84
31. What in the World Is the World? — 88
32. For the Love of a Hundred-Dollar Bill — 91
33. The Pathways to Progress in Faith — 94
34. Why the Opposite of Love Is Not Hate but Fear — 97
35. We Hate because He First Hated Us — 100
36. The Most Important Word in the Bible — 104
37. Why Trouble Is Not a Problem — 107
38. Ladies and Gentlemen of the Jury . . . — 110
39. On Playing the God Card . . . — 112
40. Why We've Gotten Eternal Life Wrong — 116
41. Why Discipleship Is Not Preparation for Eternal Life — 121
42. Getting on with the Gospel — 125
43. Could the New Testament Be Wrong? — 127
44. Why the Last Words May Be the Most Important Words — 129

The Sower's Creed — 132

Introduction

"Where is He who has been born King of the Jews? For we saw His star in the east and have come to worship Him."

—Matthew 2:2 (NASB)

I remember as a child the first time my father showed me the Big Dipper. With the lights from town dim in the distance, we looked into the vast expanse of uncountable stars in the clear, crisp night sky. "There's the Big Dipper," he quietly remarked. Having no idea what he meant, I inquired, "What's the Big Dipper?"

He said it was a constellation; a collection of stars that formed the shape of a large ladle, or dipper. Then he took my hand and extended it toward the sky with his as he traced the shape of the seven stars that made up the dipper. Wow! How had I missed it before? The better question is, How on earth would I have ever seen it had someone not pointed it out to me?

Now that I saw them, those stars seemed to shine brighter than the others around them. It gave me that feeling of being on the inside of something. In the midst of literally billions on billions of constantly shining stars, I now knew one of the great secrets of the universe.

It's amazing how we can look at something endlessly and not really see it, and once we finally do, we can't miss it. It was there all the time, beckoning to us, waiting on us to have eyes to see.

As it is with the stars, so it can be with Scripture—726,109 words (or stars) come together to form this ancient text arranging themselves in 31,102 distinct constellations, or verses. These constellations order themselves into sixty-six different galaxies, or books of the Bible. All of these galaxies together make up an intricate universe of wisdom and an expansive array of revealed truth, every jot and tittle of which tells the story of the God of heaven and earth.

"The heavens declare the glory of God," sings the psalmist, "the skies proclaim the work of his hands. Day after day they pour forth speech; night after night they reveal knowledge" (Ps. 19:1–2). Despite this, one can gaze at the pages of this magisterial book and miss its essential meaning. Someone must take our hand and with theirs trace the ancient constellations for our eyes to see. That's what the inspired writers of Scripture do.

Near the end of the Bible is a short sermon of profound consequence. It has come to be called 1 John. Penned by the apostle John, author of the gospel that also bears his name, this little book traces the arc of a series of giant constellations that together illuminate the intergalactic wonders of the entire universe.

My father revealed another awe-inspiring feature hidden in the brilliance of the night sky that night. He showed me how the last two stars on the ladle end of the constellation aligned to point to another star. He called it the "North Star." He told me from ancient times, when a person was lost at sea or in the woods at night they could find the seven stars of the Big Dipper, and by tracing a line through the last two stars they could locate the North Star. With north in sight, it was easy for them to locate south, east, and west as well.

There's a short phrase repeatedly echoing through the pages of this first epistle of John. Each time it begins with these words, "This is how we know." We see it at least half a dozen times. "[This is how] we know that we have come to know him" (2:3); "This is how we know that we belong to the truth" (3:19); "This is how we know that we live in him and he in us" (4:13); and "This is how we know that we love the children of God" (5:2). It is as though John were holding our hand, tracing these constellations of revelation with his finger for our eyes to see.

In one way or another we can trace them all back to the constellation pointing us to them in the first place: John 3:16. If Scripture has a Big Dipper, this is it. "For God so loved the world that he gave his one and only Son, that whoever believes in him shall not perish but have eternal life." This is the introduction to the gospel; what we might call the first half. In the most interesting way, these stars align to point us toward true north, orienting our lifelong journey to the gospel's conclusion, or the second half. "This is how we know what love is: Jesus Christ laid down his life for us. And we ought to lay down our lives for our brothers and sisters" (1 John 3:16).

In this edition of the Daily Text we will walk and work our way through 1 John. Each chapter picks up the Scripture text where the last left off. In like fashion, each chapter offers a short reflection on the text along with a prayer and a question for the soul's searching. Some will want to read a chapter a day while others may choose to read a series of chapters at a time. My only request is that you read it together with others. After all, this is how we know.

As we embark, let us do so with the mind and heart of those ancient sky-gazing kings who first followed the star to Bethlehem. "Where is He who has been born King of the Jews? For we saw His star in the east and have come to worship Him" (Matt. 2:2 NASB).

1 | I Believe John

1 JOHN 1:1–4 | That which was from the beginning, which we have heard, which we have seen with our eyes, which we have looked at and our hands have touched—this we proclaim concerning the Word of life. The life appeared; we have seen it and testify to it, and we proclaim to you the eternal life, which was with the Father and has appeared to us. We proclaim to you what we have seen and heard, so that you also may have fellowship with us. And our fellowship is with the Father and with his Son, Jesus Christ. We write this to make our joy complete.

Consider This

John still can't wrap his mind around what happened. It is as though he speaks these words aloud so his own ears can hear them. The curious and almost cryptic trilogy of phrases, "the Word of life," "the life," and "the eternal life," reach to grasp a heretofore-unprecedented category of reality. When a human being passes through death and comes out on the other side even more alive than before, we have an indescribable situation.

"He is risen indeed," just doesn't do it justice.

Someone so completely human yet unutterably divine cannot be comprehended; one can only behold him. It leaves an eyewitness saying to himself as well as to his listeners something akin to, "If I hadn't seen and heard and touched him with my own hands, I wouldn't believe it either."

And this is the challenge of Easter. That Jesus was raised from the dead can never be proved; only believed.

You ask me how I know he lives? John. I believe John.

The Prayer

Almighty God, thank you for eyewitnesses to the miracle of your Son. Thank you for inspiring them to write it down. And thank you for the millions of disciples who have given themselves and, at times, their lives to get this revelation to us. Come, Holy Spirit, and usher us into the fellowship of the Father and the Son and reveal to us through John's letter the indescribable mystery of the gospel. In Jesus' name. Amen.

The Question

What difference does it make to you that our faith is founded on the testimony of actual eyewitnesses and not merely on our own spiritual experience?

2 The Seduction of the Middle

gospel light bearing

1 JOHN 1:5–7 | This is the message we have heard from him and declare to you: God is (light) in him there is no darkness at all. If we claim to have fellowship with him and yet walk in the darkness, we lie and do not live out the truth. But if we walk in the light, as he is in the light, we have fellowship with one another, and the blood of Jesus, his Son, purifies us from all sin.

Consider This

John shoots straight. We need that in times like these. Light or darkness. Truth or lies. Fellowship or isolation. I appreciate the simplicity of these binary terms. We live in an age that hungers for a third option, a middle way, an in-between place.

No one wants darkness, but we will readily settle for less than pure light. It results in dimness. No one wants lies, but we will willingly accept something for less than pure truth. It results in the confusion of compromise. No one wants isolation, but we will graciously make do with less-than-real relationships. It results in crowdsourced anonymity. *To much light is blinding*

Cutting to the chase: we want our relationship with God to be independent of our relationships with other people. We also want it to be defined more by the quantity of our quiet times than the quality of our relationships.

John will not have it. We want to believe a living relationship with God is possible while our relationships with other people languish. Perhaps the biggest misconception we have is that our relationship with God will determine our relationships with other people. It's just the opposite. If you want to know what kind of fellowship I have with God, examine my relationships with other people.

If I do not have fellowship with, say, my wife, I am not walking in the light. The extent to which I am willing to ignore the problem is the extent to which I am willing to live isolated in the dimly lit shadows of half-truths. What is a shadow but a shade from darkness? What is a half-truth but a lie by another name? Something deep within the human condition doesn't want black or white. We crave fifty shades of gray.

Thank God for John, who loves us too much to leave us in the comfortable death trap of neither here nor there, in the lukewarm water of somewhere in between.

John shoots straight. We need that in times like these.

The Prayer

Heavenly Father, thank you for inspiring these un-minced words from John. Reveal to me the mushy, undefined middle places in my life. In particular, turn your searchlight onto my relationships. Show me where I need to make amends. Come, Holy Spirit, and show me the way to walk in the Light. In Jesus' name. Amen.

The Question

What relationships in your life are compromised or broken at present? What might this be telling you about your relationship with God?

The Antidote to Self-Deception

1 JOHN 1:8 | If we claim to be without sin, we deceive ourselves and the truth is not in us.

Consider This

The longer I live, the more I realize we human beings have an almost limitless capacity to deceive ourselves. In other words, sin may not be our biggest problem. I'm beginning to think our biggest problem is the way we deceive ourselves *about* sin.

I'll go first. Like you, I probably wouldn't come out and claim to be without sin. My problem is the way I have slowly adopted patterns of sin in my own life that I don't even see as sin anymore. They have become my normal.

For instance, I remember a time in my past when I was a fiercely analytical, point-out-the-problem kind of person. I considered it a gift. I had what I considered the spiritual gift of figuring out what was wrong with just about anything—including you. One day, by the mercy of God, the Holy Spirit revealed to me that I had a critical spirit. What I had normalized as the "gift of critical analysis" was actually the sin of a critical spirit.

Translation: I was self-deceived. I hurt people with impunity. The real bottom line? This was a failure to love. In my judgment, John's greatest gift to us will be the ability to understand sin through the lens of our relationships rather than through the metrics of our personal performance. Lots more on that to come.

If we claim to be without sin, we deceive ourselves and the truth is not in us.

Here is a walking-around prayer as we walk this way with John. It's something of an antidote to self-deception: "Lord Jesus Christ, Son of God, have mercy on me a sinner."

See what I mean? More on this tomorrow.

The Prayer

Lord Jesus, I confess I am a sinner. Now would you help me to actually confess my sins, and not just the outward behaviors, but the inward dispositions and broken ways of my life? Help me to understand sin not as my failure to live up to my standards, but as my failure to love you and other people. In your name, Lord. Amen.

The Question

What is the difference between identifying yourself as a sinner and actually confessing your sins?

4 Dealing with the Biggest "If" in Life

1 JOHN 1:8–10 | If we claim to be without sin, we deceive ourselves and the truth is not in us. If we confess our sins, he is faithful and just and will forgive us our sins and purify us from all unrighteousness. If we claim we have not sinned, we make him out to be a liar and his word is not in us.

Consider This

If yesterday's lesson was "Self-deception makes us immune from the truth," today's lesson is "Self-awareness opens the way for the truth to set us free."

If we confess our sins, he is faithful and just and will forgive us our sins and purify us from all unrighteousness.

John is giving us a major insight into both the broken nature of people and the merciful nature of God. The nature and character of God is beautifully and perfectly seen in Jesus Christ. He is "faithful and just" and forgiving in a way that actually changes us.

We simply cannot purify ourselves from "all unrighteousness," but Jesus can. While we cannot purify ourselves, we do have the power in our will to prevent it from happening. Perhaps the most critical word in today's text, from verse 9, is "if."

"If we confess our sins." Everything hinges on this massive "if." Of course, we learn in verse 8 that the reason we fail to confess our sins is because we have lost awareness of them. They are who we have become. Over the course of long periods of time, we ever so slowly walk away from God. The gospel of Jesus Christ says that even if we are a million miles away, one simple act can restore us to the immediate blessing of fellowship with God. "If we confess our sins."

It's a catch-22 though. How can we confess our sins if we have no sense of them? How can we confess our sins if our hearts have become hardened to them? Here's my take: confession doesn't begin with naming our sins. It begins with claiming the truth that we are sinners. Remember: we aren't sinners because we sin. We sin because we are sinners. That word "sinner" is loaded with all kinds of shame-filled baggage. To identify myself as a sinner is not to heap shame on myself. It's the only way to become free of shame. To identify myself as a sinner is the first step on the journey to becoming aware of my sins. Finally, to identify myself as a sinner is the only way to be not only cleansed from sin but progressively set free from it.

Because of the finished work of Jesus Christ through his death, resurrection, and ascension, sin has lost its power. Be clear, though: sin will not go away quietly. It's no match for the power of the grace of God in Jesus Christ, but we have a clear role to play in the process. It will come down to one big "if."

The Prayer

Lord Jesus, help me understand that I am not a sinner because I sin but that I sin because I am a sinner. Humble me with the self-awareness of the brokenness of my identity that I might learn to humble myself and so rise up into the wholeness of who you say I am and are making me to become. In your name, Jesus. Amen.

The Question

What difference do you think it makes—this notion of sinning because we are sinners rather than the other way around? Why does this matter?

On Preachers and Sermons versus Communicators and Messages

1 JOHN 1:8–10 ᴋᴊ21 | If we say that we have no sin, we deceive ourselves and the truth is not in us. If we confess our sins, He is faithful and just to forgive us our sins, and to cleanse us from all unrighteousness. If we say that we have not sinned, we make Him a liar, and His Word is not in us.

Consider This

Rather than a letter, 1 John is actually a sermon. What is the purpose of a sermon? A sermon is a very distinctive and unique form of communication; at least it should be. It's not a lecture or a motivational speech or a keynote address or a good old-fashioned scolding. And while a sermon often offers teaching, this is not its primary purpose.

The purpose of a sermon is to bring hearers into an experiential encounter with the living God. A sermon, properly prepared and proclaimed in the power of the Holy Spirit, aspires to lift its hearers into the realm of divine revelation.

Good preaching does not aim to get us to sit up straight and take notes as though we were in a classroom. No, true preaching causes us to lean forward in humble expectation of hearing a word from God. A real sermon brings us into a keen awareness of the already-present presence of God through an encounter with the Word of God proclaimed in the power of the Spirit of God.

Note, this is not about the preacher. When what I have described actually happens, people will approach the preacher after a sermon and tell him or her things they heard from God, causing that preacher to go away scratching his or her head because he or she didn't actually say those things. People will say things like, "It felt like you were talking directly to me," when the preacher had no idea you were even there.

True preaching is an event like none other. The outcome of this kind of preaching is that people, the broken image-bearers of God, will be reconciled to the Father, progressively restored to the image of Jesus Christ, and constrained by the Holy Spirit—empowered by the love of God to fully participate in the mission of God in the world. That, my friends, is what the supernatural speech we call a sermon is designed to do.

So, what does this have to do with today's text? Thanks for asking. Remember, 1 John is a sermon. Recall the text we have been living with the past few days:

> If we say that we have no sin, we deceive ourselves and the truth is not in us. If we confess our sins, He is faithful and just to forgive us our sins, and to cleanse us from all unrighteousness. If we say that we have not sinned, we make Him a liar, and His Word is not in us.

These days I think we hear far more messages delivered by communicators than we hear sermons proclaimed by preachers. What's the difference? Most messages (and I've preached my fair share of them) either inform us, entertain us, shame us, or worst of all, bore us. A message may lead us to make admissions about ourselves or increase our resolve. Sermons can compel us to authentic confession that will cause us to be changed from one degree of glory to the next (see 1 Corinthians 3).

That last little phrase may capture it best. A sermon has the mysterious capacity to impart God's Word to us in a way that gets God's Word in us. John skips the introductory niceties and funny stories, and by the time he gets to the seventh sentence, he's into the gospel. In the document we call 1 John is a sermon on the Word of God that itself is the Word of God. It's awe-inspiring.

Let's lean forward together and see where this goes.

The Prayer

Father, thank you for inspiring this ancient sermon from John and for preserving it through every generation since. Because of your inspiration, it speaks as clearly and pointedly as it did from its first speaking. Open my ears and my eyes and cause me to lean into it, not as an ancient letter but as the living and active Word of God for us today. We pray in Jesus' name. Amen.

The Question

How do you see the difference between a sermon and a lecture and between a preacher and teacher?

6 Reframing Sin

1 JOHN 2:1 KJ21 | My little children, these things write I unto you, that ye sin not. And if any man sin, we have an advocate with the Father, Jesus Christ the righteous.

Consider This

Is this possible? To not sin.

As I read John, I don't think he means sinlessness or some kind of flawless perfection. I think he's getting at what it means to be made perfect in love. Sin, for John, is disobedience to the singular command of Jesus. What is that command?

"My command is this: Love each other as I have loved you" (John 15:12).

This means disobedience to Jesus can always be brought back to this one thing: the failure to "love each other as I have loved you." Could it really be this simple? Sin is the failure to love other people in the way Jesus loves us.

To be made perfect in love means growing in the love of God for other people. I have typically thought of sin as doing something wrong. What if I thought instead of sin as doing harm to other people? It ceases to be so much about *my failure* and a lot more about *their pain*.

What if to "not sin" isn't all about managing my behavior but is rather about consistently and progressively extending myself in love for other people?

John Wesley had a lot to say about this. In fact, 1 John was among his very favorite books in the Bible. In a letter he composed on the subject, he put it like this:

Entire sanctification, or Christian perfection, is neither more nor less than pure love; love expelling sin, and governing both the heart and life of a child of God. The Refiner's fire purges out all that is contrary to love, and that many times by a pleasing smart. Leave all this to Him that does all things well, and that loves you better than you do yourself.[1]

My little children, these things write I unto you, that ye sin not.

---

1. John Wesley, *The Complete Works of John Wesley*, vol. 12, *Letters*, Letters to Mr. Walter Churchey, of Brecon, February 21, 1771 (Albany, OR: The Ages Digital Library Collections, 1996, 1997), online at http://www.briarchasechurch.org/V6F-Z /WES_WW12.PDF.

John saw the possibility of life on another plane—of "on earth as it is in heaven" (Matt. 6:10). Do you believe it is possible?

The Prayer

Abba Father, I confess that, instead of believing in the possibility of the power of your love, I have readily settled for the predictability of sin. I confess that I have chosen to see sin more in the light of its impact on me than its injury to others. For these reasons I have come to tolerate sin as the inevitable destiny of my life. Come, Holy Spirit, and deliver me from this self-centered vision, which blinds me from seeing others. We pray in Jesus' name. Amen.

The Question

What if we began to see sin less as our moral failure and more as our callous disregard of other people?

7 The Game-Changing Question of Easter

1 JOHN 2:1–2 | My dear children, I write this to you so that you will not sin. But if anybody does sin, we have an advocate with the Father—Jesus Christ, the Righteous One. He is the atoning sacrifice for our sins, and not only for ours but also for the sins of the whole world.

Consider This

I still can't get over this. John seems to think it is possible to "not sin." In my years of following Jesus, I don't have a memory of anyone who actually believed that. I have met countless people who believe Jesus Christ is the atoning sacrifice for our sins.

So does it follow that since Jesus Christ atones for our sin (and that he will readily forgive us when we sin), we don't need to worry about *not* sinning? I mean, of course it would be *nice* to not sin, but is it really essential? This is the same kind of question believers were asking in the early days (and ever since). In Paul's letter to the Roman church he responds like this:

> What shall we say, then? Shall we go on sinning so that grace may increase? By no means! We are those who have died to sin; how can we live in it any longer? Or don't you know that all of us who were baptized into Christ Jesus were baptized into his death? We were therefore buried with him through baptism into death in order that, just as Christ was raised from the dead through the glory of the Father, we too may live a new life. (Rom. 6:1–4)

Go back and read that again. The writers of the New Testament make an extraordinary claim here. They contend we are dead to sin.

So, I ask you (and me), "Are we dead to sin?" This is the post-Easter question. We must reckon with the answer to this question, and until we do, we will be hopelessly compromised. When Paul says, "In the same way, count yourselves dead to sin but alive to God in Christ Jesus" (Rom. 6:11), this is what he is talking about.

Most of us are good with the death and resurrection of Jesus being the atonement for our sins. When it comes to his death and resurrection being the power to not sin, it's a different story. Why is that? It requires nothing of us to be "saved by grace through faith" except faith (Eph. 2:8 HCSB). But once we are "saved by grace through faith," our faith must go to work. We must act on the grace we have received. We must, as Paul will say later, "put [sin] to death" (Col. 3:5).

So, getting back to the big question, Is it possible to not sin? What if we flipped that question on its side and asked it like this: Is it possible to love?

I'm going to begin asking myself that question in the midst of my daily situations (when I'm on the verge of being infuriated). Is it possible, in this situation, to love? I think that's the question the Holy Spirit waits to hear, ever ready not only with the answer but the creativity and the power to respond.

I think that question just might be a game changer.

The Prayer

Lord Jesus, thank you for being our Advocate with the Father. Thank you for the new and living way you have opened up for us. Fill us with the Holy Spirit that we might live into the birthright of our second birth—the power to truly love others. Take us past our superficial understanding of sin as our personal failure and reveal to us the way our sin actually harms others. Then show us what love looks like in those moments. We pray in your name, Jesus. Amen.

The Question

Find a garden-variety sin in your life (e.g., anger, impatience, etc.) and think through all the ways it does harm to others. What would it mean to reframe this sin as the failure to love in these instances? This will not come naturally or easily. Stay with it.

8 Love Is Not Soft; It's Hard

1 JOHN 2:3–6 HCSB | This is how we are sure that we have come to know Him: by keeping His commands. The one who says, "I have come to know Him," yet doesn't keep His commands, is a liar, and the truth is not in him. But whoever keeps His word, truly in him the love of God is perfected. This is how we know we are in Him: The one who says he remains in Him should walk just as He walked.

Consider This

I don't know about you, but I can't remember the last time I heard a sermon like this one. John is not pulling any punches.

Here's a rough paraphrase:

> I'm not going to ask you if you "know God." I don't
> need to ask that question, because your answer is
> irrelevant. There's a way I can find out if you know
> God and I don't even have to bother you. I will just
> start watching you from a distance and see if you are
> keeping God's commands. If, in fact, you are keeping
> God's commands, I will know that you know God.

He doesn't stop there though. More paraphrase: "Now, if you tell me you know God and it turns out you don't keep his commands, then there's a technical term for you: a liar. You are a liar and your life is devoid of the truth."

How's that for an eye-stick? It's as though John is grabbing us by the shoulders and shaking us a bit. It's actually a pretty merciful gesture when you think about it. If a person thinks he or she knows God, but doesn't, that is one self-deceived individual.

OK, so what does it mean to keep God's commands? As we will see, John brings it back to the issue of our relationships and the presence of love therein. I'm getting some pushback (which I always appreciate) on this issue of love, with claims that this is flimsy, soft, relativistic, and that I'm missing the mark when it comes to the way I'm defining sin—which incidentally means "missing the mark."

So, I ask you: What is the mark? I think the mark is the holy love of God.

When I talk about love, I get the impression some think I'm going soft on sin. I'll grant you that the word *love* has been decimated in the present age, but I don't think there's a better word. In order to make a distinction, I am using *holy* alongside *love* to indicate virtuous activity of another order entirely. The way I mean to talk about love has nothing to do with love being soft. No, quite the contrary, love is hard. Look at how the second half of today's text describes it.

But whoever keeps His word, truly in him the love of God is perfected. This is how we know we are in Him: The one who says he remains in Him should walk just as He walked.

This is not about playing nice. We are talking about nothing less than taking on the supernatural nature of Jesus Christ by the power of the Holy Spirit so that we can live a new life. The ongoing reality of salvation is not about WWJD. It's more like, HDJDI: How did Jesus do it? The reality of the resurrection means the resources available to Jesus are now available to us. Because Jesus died for our sins, we are dead to sin. Because the love of God raised Jesus to life, we are alive to holy love. Love is not an emotion. It is a supernatural power always creating the possibility to overcome sin by the holiness of God. It's *why* John writes, "My dear children, I write this to you so that you will not sin" (2:1).

The Prayer

Lord Jesus, I want to be one who keeps your commands, yet I know it is impossible to do so without your constant help. I need a new center of gravity, which is the power of your love. Lead me into the hardness of love that I might learn to trust you more deeply, until your love is my love.

Come, Holy Spirit, and make the possible probable in my life.
In your name, Jesus. Amen.

The Question

How does this litmus test of obedience to God's commands
being the evidence of our knowing God or not strike you?
How does your life stand up to the test?

9 Love Cannot Be Taught; Only Demonstrated

1 JOHN 2:7–8 HCSB | Dear friends, I am not writing you a new
command but an old command that you have had from the
beginning. The old command is the message you have heard.
Yet I am writing you a new command, which is true in Him and
in you, because the darkness is passing away and the true light
is already shining.

Consider This

John sounds a bit like Master Yoda today. Passing away, the
darkness is. Already shining, the truth is now.

How can something be both new and old at the same time.
Nothing stays new. In the season of spring, everything is
new again, but it never stays that way. Early spring always
reminds me of my favorite poem. It's called "Nothing Gold
Can Stay," by Robert Frost.

Nature's first green is gold,
Her hardest hue to hold.
Her early leaf's a flower;
But only so an hour.
Then leaf subsides to leaf.
So Eden sank to grief,
So dawn goes down to day.
Nothing gold can stay.
(public domain)

The command John will continue to drive home is not a new command. It's actually an old command. Even when Jesus told his disciples he was giving them a "new command" (John 13:34), it was still as old as Leviticus (see 19:18). In the old days, they wanted to interpret this text about loving one's neighbor as they loved themselves in the sense of what is required to fulfill one's obligation to the law or their duty. It's why the Pharisee pressed Jesus with the question, "Who is my neighbor?" (Luke 10:29). He wanted to know the boundaries or limits of this law concerning neighbor love. He was looking for an interpretation. Rather than giving an interpretation, Jesus told the now-famous story about the good Samaritan. Instead of opting for what is required, Jesus chose to emphasize what was possible.

Yet I am writing you a new command, which is true in Him and in you . . .

When Jesus wanted to teach his disciples the meaning of love, he didn't render an interpretation. He became the interpretation. He washed their feet. This command to love others is an old commandment, but every time someone actually dares to obey it, things are made new. In organizations, relationships, communities, and even nations, the love of God revealed by Jesus Christ and now manifested in and through his people makes things new.

Holy love means treating people extravagantly, according to their best interests, rather than handling them according to the calculus of our best interests. Jesus' death on the cross was clearly not in his best interest. He asked for the cup of suffering to pass him by, yet for the sake of love, he became "obedient unto death" (Phil. 2:8 KJ21). As a result, the new creation broke in on the old, broken one. Everything is being made new. The old is passing away. The new is breaking forth.

Every time we love others as Jesus has loved us, even in the smallest of ways, the new creation is extended further. This, in effect, pushes the darkness back. As we will see tomorrow, this is what it means to "walk in the light, as he is in the light" (1 John 1:7).

Passing away, the darkness is. Already shining, the truth is now. Stay gold.

The Prayer

Lord Jesus, thank you for making all things new. Thank you for making me new. Fill me with fresh faith to grasp this unshakable truth—your love is making me new. I welcome the power of your holy love to make me the kind of person whose love makes others new. Yes, Lord, you can do this. We pray in your name, Jesus. Amen.

The Question

What if you came to clearly see the self-interested nature of your own ways of loving others and began to fathom the power of love when it becomes truly self-giving and authentically interested in others? What would that mean for you? Would you ask the Holy Spirit to reveal to you the hold that your self-interest has on you when it comes to your relationships with other people?

Lost Is Not a Subjective Feeling; It's an Objective Reality

1 JOHN 2:9–11 ESV | Whoever says he is in the light and hates his brother is still in darkness. Whoever loves his brother abides in the light, and in him there is no cause for stumbling. But whoever hates his brother is in the darkness and walks in the darkness, and does not know where he is going, because the darkness has blinded his eyes.

Consider This

I will never forget it. I was about sixteen and headed to the woods after school, as was my practice, to hunt deer. At dusk a young buck walked along a ridge nearby. I took aim and fired. The deer fled. *How could I have missed?* I thought to myself. I began walking through the woods in search of this animal. Just as I was about to give up, I spotted the deer in the distance. I had been successful with my shot only to realize I had a bigger problem now. It was dark and I was lost. I frantically walked in one direction, to no avail. Then I walked in another direction, again to no avail. Then I lost track of the deer and began in desperation to try to refind him, which I did. I was literally walking around in darkness. I had no idea where I was going. The darkness had blinded me.

Being lost is not primarily a subjective experience. It is an objective reality. I am not lost because I "feel" lost. I am lost because I am walking around in darkness and have no idea where I am going or how to get there. The thing about being lost is you don't realize you are lost until it's too late. The truth for me that night in the woods? I was lost long before I realized it.

John once again shoots straight. He's not asking people whether they are walking in darkness. He is looking at their relationships. He says, in effect, our relationship with God is about as good as our worst relationship with other people. That's hard to swallow. I so want to assess my own walk with God according to how near I feel to God. Am I spending time in God's Word? Am I spending time in prayer? Am I sharing in fellowship with other believers? Am I taking care of those in need? These are the ways I want to measure the state of my relationship with God.

John will not have it. He says we can read and pray and fast and study and do good and be in small groups until the cows come home and it won't matter one whit if we are not loving our brothers and sisters around us. Remember: love is not a feeling or affection for John. Biblical love means putting the needs of others above my own self-interest. Neither is hatred a feeling for John. Hatred is not so much raging animosity toward others as it is our indifference to or neglect of their need. There is no middle ground here. You either love others by putting their interests above your own, or you don't—which means, in John's inspired vision, that you hate them.

I'm going to put this into the most unvarnished language I can come up with. To the extent that I am not actively putting my self-interest aside and serving and helping and looking out for the best interest of the people around me, I am walking around in the darkness, lost as I can be. It doesn't matter if I feel lost or not. It doesn't matter if I can talk a good game or preach a good sermon or lead a good Bible study or do a good mission project or anything else. If I am not actively caring for the people around me, I am lost.

I hate to say it that way, but I do think this is what John is telling us.

The smartest thing I did that dark night when I was lost in the woods was to admit that I was lost, at which point I stopped walking around. I sat down and I prayed for the mercy of God in the form of someone coming to find me. And that's what happened. I will always remember my first glimpse of the flickering flashlight winding its way through the thick forest in the hands of my father, who had come to find me.

I'm feeling as if I may need to sit down right where I am and roll through my relational Rolodex—even just the people I see on a daily and weekly basis.

Let me be clear in closing. Loving other people is not the condition for salvation. It's the confirming sign of it. (I don't have a relationship with God because I say I do or because I feel as though I do or because I've prayed the right prayer.) Do I make those relationships about others, or is it all about me? There's your sign.

The Prayer

Lord Jesus, I will open myself and just ask you: Am I lost? Am I walking around in darkness without even knowing it? I open myself to the possibility this could be true. Come, Holy Spirit, turn on the lights, and search me out. Even more, give me a glimpse of your power and possibility to really change and grow. I ask it in your name, Jesus. Amen.

The Question

What is at stake if someone is lost and does not know it and is not open to realizing it? What keeps you from honestly opening yourself up to a few other people along these lines? What if it takes others to help you find your way?

1 When Sin Gets Redefined as Not Sin

1 JOHN 2:12–14 |

I am writing to you, dear children,

because your sins have been forgiven on account
of his name.

I am writing to you, fathers,

because you know him who is from the beginning.

I am writing to you, young men,

because you have overcome the evil one.

I write to you, dear children,

because you know the Father.

I write to you, fathers,

because you know him who is from the beginning.

I write to you, young men,

because you are strong,

and the word of God lives in you,

and you have overcome the evil one.

Consider This

In some ways this passage feels like a "Now for something completely different" text. On a second pass, though, it
strikes me as a reassuring pastoral move.

Think about it. John came straight out of the bull pen with guns blazing. It's as if he had a major ax to grind with somebody. After examining today's text, it's all coming together for me.

We need to remember something about the nature of sermons. On the one hand, to the extent a sermon's architecture is formed by the Word of God, it is timeless. On the other hand, a sermon is always spoken into a particular context, addressing a particular people who are dealing with particular issues and challenges. On this point, we must explore the translatability of the message from the first century to (in our case) the twenty-first century. The parallels and points of application are enormous.

I think John's coming out so strident in this sermon was more about crushing the ideas of the false teachers who were influencing the people than it was aimed at the people themselves. Someone had been teaching these followers of Jesus some version of a cheap-grace gospel. What do I mean by this? I think these teachers were soft-pedaling the gravity of sin as though it didn't matter anymore. They believed that because of the work of Jesus, they had a license to do whatever seemed right to them, no matter its impact on others. Said another way, these false teachers basically taught the followers of Jesus that because of Jesus' finished work, they were finished with sin. Here lies the subtle seduction of false teaching. It's true that because of Jesus' finished work on the cross, we who place our faith in him are finished with sin. The problem is, sin is not finished with us. It has not gone away, nor has sin somehow been reclassified as not sin, which seems to be the essence of the false teaching. All people needed was some claim of knowing Jesus and nothing else mattered. Go back and reread the sermon up to the point of today's text and see if you agree with my hypothesis.

John takes the proverbial bull by the horns: he says we must call sin "sin"; confess our sins; receive God's forgiveness; and lean further into the grace of God. The sign of salvation's authenticity is the ever-increasing obedience of holy love, which can only be witnessed in the midst of human relationships. "They will know we are Christians" by our T-shirts? Not a chance. It will be by our love (John 13:35).

John wasn't holding a mirror up in front of the people and calling them liars for the ways they failed to love one another. John told them the love of God could cleanse them from the effects of sin and deliver them from the power of sin. The love of God could bring them into relationships with other people in such a way that their lives exuded the joy-filled, holy love of God, which is the power of the gospel of Jesus Christ that can take a broken world and transform it into a new creation.

False teaching is as present today as it ever has been. It must be confronted because of its seductive and even compelling allure to redefine sin as not sin. When we do that, it is like ignoring the diagnosis of an aggressively metastasizing cancer and pretending it's not there, all the while claiming to know the doctor, as though that knowledge will somehow cure our disease. Sin, like cancer, destroys the body from the inside out. That's what it does to people, to relationships, and to communities. Sin is not a problem for God. Self-deception is the big problem because it immunizes us from the cure of confession. In short, when sin gets redefined as "not sin," all hell breaks loose.

OK. We are in pretty deep now. How do we put some punctuation on this and get on with today? I felt that we needed that context to better understand today's text, but let's wrap up with a comment about today's text.

In today's text, John is reassuring the flock. He frames the way of salvation not as a sin-free path, but as a sin-defeating journey, a journey in which we can be secure in the grace of God just as we are, while confident that the love of God will not leave us just as we are. Just as a child grows into a young man or woman and later into the ripe maturity of old age, so the power of God will prosper us through every stage of faith and life, transforming us from one degree of glory to the next until our image reflects his likeness, as in a mirror.

It has been called the royal way of the holy cross. As Steven Curtis Chapman put it so well in one of his songs, there's "no better place on earth than the road that leads to heaven."[2]

The Prayer

Lord Jesus, would you take me beyond the doctrine of my confession and reveal to me the doctrine of my real life? What do my real life and my real relationships reveal that I believe? Come, Holy Spirit. Expose and root out any false teaching that has lodged itself in my soul. Something tells me a breakthrough could be near. In your name, Jesus. Amen.

The Question

Are you growing? Or has your growth become arrested? How might you become more honest with yourself? How can you enlist the help of others? What if you don't do this?

2 Why the Problem Is Not Pornography

1 JOHN 2:15–17 ᴋᴊ21 | Love not the world, neither the things that are in the world. If any man love the world, the love of the Father is not in him. For all that is in the world—the lust of the flesh, and the lust of the eyes, and the pride of life—is not of the Father, but is of the world. And the world passeth away and the lust thereof, but he that doeth the will of God abideth for ever.

Consider This

The power of human desire cannot be contained, but by the mercy of God, it can be trained. One of the great traps in a text like today's is to interpret John to say, "Have nothing to do with the world." It gets further translated into such helpful sayings as "Don't drink, smoke, chew, or run with those who do." The next thing you know, we have a full-blown theology of holiness that leads to withdrawing from anything that even smacks of the world. Being holy becomes far more about being disassociated from the world than being distinctive within it.

It seems right, but it's dead wrong. John doesn't say to have nothing to do with the world. He says do not love the world. You see our big mistake when it comes to the way we think about the world is we think the world is "out there." The truth? The world is "in here"—in us.

For all that is in the world—the lust of the flesh, and the lust of the eyes, and the pride of life—is not of the Father, but is of the world.

The world John speaks of is not some adult bookstore on the side of the freeway. It's the broken desires in the depths of our hearts. The R-rated movie is not the problem. It's the broken place in me that desires to see something salacious that is the real issue. The "lust of the flesh, and the lust of the eyes, and the pride of life" is just another way of describing undiscipled desire. The issue is not my materialistic neighbors; it's my covetousness. When you boil it all down, the problem is never really out there in the so-called world. The problem is in here, in the broken world of my inmost self.

Thinking the world is out there rather than within us explains how some of the most strident opponents of sin are the most secret sinners. Ironically, often the greatest crusaders against online pornography are some of the most perverse participants in it. They thought the problem was online when all the while it was inside. It's not about the pornography out there but the perversion in here.

Real discipleship in the tradition of Jesus is not about trying to manage sin by running away from the world. It's about the conversion of our deepest desires within it. The only way to stop loving the world is to be seized by and given to a far greater affection: the holy love of God. Real discipleship is not the moral crusade to manage sin. It's training the heart by the power of the Word of God and the Spirit of God to desire what is truly good and beautiful and holy and loving—to desire God alone.

The Prayer

Lord Jesus, give me the courage to stop identifying sin out there and become honest about the source of sin in here, within me. Save me from the trap of self-shaming, which takes me away from the cross. Come, Holy Spirit, and cause me to run to the cross. I want you to eradicate the deeper sin in me. Change me from the inside out. In your name, Jesus. Amen.

The Question

How might you get past managing your behavior to the deeper brokenness in your life? What if you became convinced that the more honest you were about yourself, the more genuinely you could know and experience the grace and love of God for yourself?

13 The Greatest Danger to the Church: Then and Now

1 JOHN 2:18–19 | Dear children, this is the last hour; and as you have heard that the antichrist is coming, even now many antichrists have come. This is how we know it is the last hour. They went out from us, but they did not really belong to us. For if they had belonged to us, they would have remained with us; but their going showed that none of them belonged to us.

Consider This

What do you think of as the greatest threat to the church of Jesus Christ? Hypocrisy? Apathy? Bad preaching? Sexual immorality? Weak faith? My take? Thanks for asking. I think it's immature faith. John is especially concerned with those who lack maturity in faith.

Allow me a brief sidebar about Christian maturity. In terms of faith, maturity has little or nothing to do with how long one has considered oneself a Christian. Many times, people who have ardently followed Jesus a short time are more mature than those who have sat around in church all their lives. Maturity is the fruit of a life consistently immersed in the Word of God and the Spirit of God. It is not signaled by a certain level of knowledge but by a growing discernment. The metric for Christian maturity is not competent skills or great gifts, but humility and holy love. The secret to maturing in Christ comes not in the quantity of Christian activity, but in the quality of one's trusting abandonment to him.

John is speaking to "children"—not kids, but people who are not yet mature in their faith. Immature faith works like a magnet to attract false teaching. It can be like a chink in the armor or a weak immune system. False teaching shipwrecks faith. The trouble with false teaching is it often has an air of plausibility to it. People not steeped in the Scripture and the Spirit are most susceptible to buying into false teaching or following after false teachers. John calls them "antichrists" because of their false teaching about Jesus Christ.

I want you to read this familiar passage of Scripture through these lenses of maturity and false teaching. This is Paul writing to the church at Ephesus:

> So Christ himself gave the apostles, the prophets, the evangelists, the pastors and teachers, to equip his people for works of service, so that the body of Christ may be built up until we all reach unity in the faith and in the knowledge of the Son of God and become mature, attaining to the whole measure of the fullness of Christ.

> Then we will no longer be infants, tossed back and forth by the waves, and blown here and there by every wind of teaching and by the cunning and craftiness of people in their deceitful scheming. Instead, speaking the truth in love, we will grow to become in every respect the mature body of him who is the head, that is, Christ. From him the whole body, joined and held together by every supporting ligament, grows and builds itself up in love, as each part does its work. (Eph. 4:11–16)

Now take a quick look at how Paul addresses this issue with the Christians at Colossae.

> So then, just as you received Christ Jesus as Lord, continue to live your lives in him, rooted and built up in him, strengthened in the faith as you were taught, and overflowing with thankfulness. See to it that no one takes you captive through hollow and deceptive philosophy, which depends on human tradition and the elemental spiritual forces of this world rather than on Christ. (Col. 2:6–8)

The greatest threat to the twenty-first-century church is the same as it was for the first-century church. Immature faith. Immature faith opens the door to false teaching. False teaching leads to false faith. It desecrates community. It destroys unity. It was a massive issue in the first century. It's going to be a major issue for the twenty-first-century church. The apostles knew what was at stake and they would not abide it. We can't either.

There's a very deadly way to attempt to combat false teaching. It's called compromise. Because false teaching destroys unity, people will often seek a compromise to recover unity. It never works. In our attempts to salvage unity in our church structures, we do grave damage to the body of Christ. There's only one way to deal with false teaching. Maturity. We must grow in maturity.

The Prayer

Lord Jesus, I will for my life to be more deeply rooted in you. I long to be established in you. Today, I am responding to your knock and opening the door to a new way of knowing you. I hold nothing back. I do not know what all this means, but I trust you. I pray in your name, Jesus. Amen.

The Question

What if you really meant that prayer? What is your next step? Where are you compromised?

4 Do You Have the Anointing?

1 JOHN 2:20–21 | But you have an anointing from the Holy One, and all of you know the truth. I do not write to you because you do not know the truth, but because you do know it and because no lie comes from the truth.

Consider This

Do you have the anointing?

Anointing. Now, there's a good old-fashioned Bible word. But what does it mean? It conjures up imagery of being anointed with oil, but that's not what this refers to. John here speaks of the inward reality of what any outward sign might point to. There's the sign and then there's the reality the sign points to. John is talking about something placed by God— the Holy One—in the inner life of a follower of Jesus.

The anointing describes the illuminated intersection of the Word of God and the Spirit of God within the life of a believer. This anointing, the holy intersection of Word and Spirit, brings us to a place of *knowing* the truth beyond mere knowledge of it. The anointing brings wisdom and discernment. The anointing is another way of saying, "Christ in you." The anointing leads us faithfully into the will of God. It is the inner instrument, the GPS, of a follower of Jesus. The anointing brings us to the sacred place Paul spoke of to the Corinthian church:

"What no eye has seen,
    what no ear has heard,
and what no human mind has conceived"—
    the things God has prepared for those who love him—

these are the things God has revealed to us by his Spirit.

The Spirit searches all things, even the deep things of God. For who knows a person's thoughts except their own spirit within them? In the same way no one knows the thoughts of God except the Spirit of God. What we have received is not the spirit of the world, but the Spirit who is from God, so that we may understand what God has freely given us. This is what we speak, not in words taught us by human wisdom but in words taught by the Spirit, explaining spiritual realities with Spirit-taught words. The person without the Spirit does not accept the things that come from the Spirit of God but considers them foolishness, and cannot understand them because they are discerned only through the Spirit. The person with the Spirit makes judgments about all things, but such a person is not subject to merely human judgments, for,

"Who has known the mind of the Lord
so as to instruct him?"
But we have the mind of Christ. (1 Cor. 2:9–16)

It's important to note here that the anointing cannot be reduced to either the Word of God or the Spirit of God, as though one without the other would suffice. I think this is the big difference between orthodoxy and heresy, between true and false teaching. On the one hand, history is littered with false teachers who claimed a subjective spiritual revelation that went beyond the objective Word of God. The Book of Mormon comes to mind. On the other hand, there has been no shortage of false teachers who claim the Spirit has revealed an interpretation or understanding of the Bible that departs from the universally established teaching of the church. In both instances we get false teaching. When John references "antichrists" in the text, he is making a direct play on words in the Greek language to define the opposite of those who have the "Chrism" or "anointing."

To grow in maturity as a follower of Jesus means to grow in the anointing. It's why false teaching is so detrimental. It leads us away from the anointing.

More than anything, God's people need to claim the anointing. This will require a fundamental training in a Word-shaped, Spirit-filled life. The anointing is the supernatural life springing forth from this kind of discipleship.

So how about it? Do you have the anointing?

The Prayer

Lord Jesus, you are the Anointed One. Thank you for the Holy Spirit, through whom you make your anointing ours. This is a miracle. Open my soul to believe it more completely and to long for it more deeply. I claim it now. I am anointed by, in, and through you. Word of God, speak. Spirit of God, fill. And all of this in the name of Jesus. Amen.

The Question

What if you began to claim, in your innermost person, the anointing of Christ in your life? What would you expect to happen? Why would you not do this?

5 The Exclusive Inclusive Gospel of Jesus Christ

1 JOHN 2:22–23 KJ21 | Who is a liar but he that denieth that Jesus is the Christ? He is antichrist who denieth the Father and the Son.

Whosoever denieth the Son, the same hath not the Father; he that acknowledgeth the Son hath the Father also.

Consider This

EXAMPLE #1: What if you had a certain kind of cancer that could only be cured with a very specific kind of medicine? What if it had a 100 percent cure rate? And what if you had access to this medicine? What if there were actually an unlimited supply of this medicine and that without this particular medicine, you would not survive the cancer? Would you take the medicine?

Of course you would.

Now, what if you found out there were people who had this kind of cancer who did not know about this lifesaving medicine? You would want to do anything you could to make sure they got the medicine, wouldn't you?

EXAMPLE #2: Jesus is the only cure for the cancer of sin. He is the only way to know the God of holy love. He will save anyone and everyone who will receive him. Those who refuse him will die in their sin.

Why is it that no one is ever offended by Example #1 and yet many are offended by Example #2? How is it that Example #2 is considered by many to be somehow unfair while Example #1 is pure good news?

Today's text makes it clear.

Whosoever denieth the Son, the same hath not the Father; he that acknowledgeth the Son hath the Father also.

John's gospel records the very words of Jesus, "I am the way and the truth and the life. No one comes to the Father except through me" (John 14:6).

The gospel of Jesus Christ is totally exclusive, yet it is radically inclusive. Anyone who will believe gets in on it.

There are a lot of people who still don't know about him yet.

The Prayer

Lord Jesus, you are the cure. Help me come to grips and own my diagnosis of sin cancer so you might apply the remedy of your grace and truth for my healing. Help me understand that sin will destroy me as cancer could, and that you are the only cure. Give me a new story, not of mere remission but of total cure. I promise to share it with others. I ask it in your name, Jesus. Amen.

The Question

What if the cure for sin cancer also has some of the discomforts that come with chemotherapy treatments to bodily cancer? Will you still pursue the treatment? What if you don't?

6 The Simple Simplicity of Abiding in the Gospel

1 JOHN 2:24–25 | As for you, see that what you have heard from the beginning remains in you. If it does, you also will remain in the Son and in the Father. And this is what he promised us—eternal life.

Consider This

If we peek behind the English text to see the Greek "codes," if you will, we see a term used no fewer than three times. The word is *meinete*. It means "abide." It often translates into English as "remain" or "dwell." John is asking his hearers to stick with the plan, to stay with the gospel as they first heard it, the pure, unadulterated gospel of Jesus Christ.

Remember: John is confronting the problem of false teaching and false teachers. He is calling a group of relatively new believers to grow up into mature faith by digging deeper into the core truth of the gospel. He instructs them to stay with it, to remain or dwell in it, to demonstrate some staying power. In short, he says to abide in the truth.

This likely reminds you of the same message in the fifteenth chapter of John:

> "I am the vine; you are the branches. If you remain in me and I in you, you will bear much fruit; apart from me you can do nothing. If you do not remain in me,

> you are like a branch that is thrown away and withers; such branches are picked up, thrown into the fire and burned. If you remain in me and my words remain in you, ask whatever you wish, and it will be done for you. This is to my Father's glory, that you bear much fruit, showing yourselves to be my disciples." (vv. 5–8)

We have one job in the life hid with Christ in God—and that is to show up, every day, day after day, and rehearse the truth that we have heard from the beginning.

My dad once shared with me a humorous strategy to ensure that he would never lose his memory. He said, "If I can wake up every day and go over the basic truth of who I am and where I am and what I'm about, then how could I ever lose my memory?" The more I think about it, the more I am convinced this is exactly what Jesus means when he says, "Abide in me." He means to wake up, day after day, rehearsing the truth of who he is and who we are and who he is to us and therefore who we can be to others.

So, what if I did that every single morning? Just this morning, I woke up a little earlier than usual (thanks to the dog) and I found myself outside, looking up at the stars. I thought to myself, *I'm going to simply remind myself of the truth of the gospel—out loud.* I went to a familiar passage of Scripture and literally declared aloud to myself (and the dog):

> John David, you have the same mind in you that was in Christ Jesus, "who, being in very nature God, did not consider equality with God something to be grasped,

but made himself nothing. And taking on the nature of a servant, and being made in human likeness and found in the appearance of a man, he humbled himself and became obedient to death, even death on a cross. Therefore, God highly exalted him and gave him the name that is above every name, that at the name of Jesus, every knee should bow in heaven, and on earth, and under the earth, and every tongue confess that Jesus Christ is Lord, to the glory of God the Father."

(That's my rendition of Philippians 2:5–11, as best as I can remember it.)

After that, I spoke aloud the Sower's Creed, as is becoming my practice (when I remember it).[3]

That was it. I didn't try to conjure up any warm, fuzzy feelings. I just dwelled in the truth of it all. I remained in the message I heard from the beginning. And I believe it changed the course of my life, just for the day. When you think about it, it's really pretty simple. How many times have I failed to simply show up because I felt as though I had to bring something special to the table, when all I had to do was show up and bring what he had already brought to me?

So, I want to encourage you today. It is all at once much easier than you think to abide in Jesus, and yet it will take all you have to simply remember and show up. He just wants us to bring his own gospel back to him. Day after day after day. The outcome will stun you. One day you will wake up and

---

3. See the back of the book for the text of the Sower's Creed.

realize you are nowhere near where you used to be, and the glory of it all is that you will realize you had nothing to do with it, other than to abide. He did everything else.

Nothing is more effective against false teaching than the simple wherewithal to do this kind of thing every single day.

The Prayer

Lord Jesus, thank you for making your gospel so clear. Thank you for the fact that we are saved not only by your death and resurrection but by your life and ascension. Thank you for the miracle and mystery of abiding in you. Would you keep clearly showing me the small part I must play in the movement and the much larger part you play? I want to know this reality more than anything. I pray in your name, Jesus. Amen.

The Question

How are you showing up every day to places of abiding in Jesus? What might change if you became more consistent in doing your small part?

17 How to Spot a Counterfeit

1 JOHN 2:26–29 | I am writing these things to you about those who are trying to lead you astray. As for you, the

anointing you received from him remains in you, and you do not need anyone to teach you. But as his anointing teaches you about all things and as that anointing is real, not counterfeit— just as it has taught you, remain in him.

And now, dear children, continue in him, so that when he appears we may be confident and unashamed before him at his coming.

If you know that he is righteous, you know that everyone who does what is right has been born of him.

Consider This

We don't need to be afraid of those who would try to lead us astray, but we must be aware of them. They are as active in the twenty-first century as they were in the first century.

One of the marks of a maturing follower of Jesus is a humble boldness born of a deep inner conviction about what is true, which consequently gives one discernment about what is false. This comes from the Holy Spirit. But how can you know it is from the Holy Spirit and that you are not being self-deceived?

Test your sense of discernment by the whole counsel of Scripture.

Is your discernment contrary to the teaching of Scripture? Does it require a stretched and strained interpretation of Scripture to reconcile with your sense of discernment? If so, there's a good chance you may be opening yourself up to false teaching. False teaching can take root so easily; through sheer strength of numbers the consensus in the present can bully the truth of the past. Never mind that it flies in the face of the truth as it has always been taught and understood for hundreds if not thousands of years.

Jesus gave some pretty explicit teaching about the Holy Spirit along these lines:

> "All this I have spoken while still with you. But the Advocate, the Holy Spirit, whom the Father will send in my name, will teach you all things and will remind you of everything I have said to you." (John 14:25–26)

> "I have much more to say to you, more than you can now bear. But when he, the Spirit of truth, comes, he will guide you into all the truth. He will not speak on his own; he will speak only what he hears, and he will tell you what is yet to come. He will glorify me because it is from me that he will receive what he will make known to you. All that belongs to the Father is mine. That is why I said the Spirit will receive from me what he will make known to you." (John 16:12–15)

The Holy Spirit is always doing a new thing, but revealing new truth? Not so much.

The best way to detect the counterfeit is not by studying counterfeits, but by studying the authentic article. It's why John insists that we stick with the message we first received—day after day after day.

The Prayer

Lord Jesus, I want to be formed by your Word and filled by your Spirit. Make me a person of clear discernment and gracious decisiveness. Protect me from false teachers and their teaching. I will not live in fear but by faith that your ability to lead me is greater than my inability to follow you as I need to. In your name I pray. Amen.

The Question

How might you more deeply open yourself up to being taught by the Word and the Spirit—not in tandem but in union? How might these moorings become deeper in your everyday life and experience? What will that require?

8 Why Attention Is More Important Than Activity

1 JOHN 3:1–3 ESV | See what kind of love the Father has given to us, that we should be called children of God; and so we are. The reason why the world does not know us is that it did not know him. Beloved, we are God's children now, and what we will be has not yet appeared; but we know that when he appears we shall be like him, because we shall see him as he is. And everyone who thus hopes in him purifies himself as he is pure.

Consider This

So much has been made over the years of the distinction between being and doing. You've heard it. "We are human beings," goes the cliché, "not human doings." We must learn to "be" before we "do."

I'm going to be frank. I think this is a completely meaningless distinction. It falls into the category of sounds good but what in the world does it mean? I mean, can you articulate it for me?

OK, so I won't just criticize without offering an alternative. I believe the alternative is in today's text. Rather than "being" and "doing," I think life comes down to "beholding" and "becoming." Allow me to develop the thought.

The first word of today's text, "See," shouldn't really have been translated "see." The Greek word there has much more force. It means "Behold." To behold something or someone is far more than to see with the naked eye. It means to perceive something with the totality of one's attention. It means to see past the surface appearance and into the very essence of reality. This word appears throughout Scripture in some very key places. It is often found on the lips of angelic beings. The word almost always signals the presence of God and points to impending divine activity or revelation.

I remember a song called "Behold What Manner of Love" that carries today's opening verse in these words: "Behold what manner of love the Father has given unto us, that we should be called the [children] of God."

This is not a nice turn of phrase. It is not a platitude. It is not a nice idea or a concept or a Hallmark card sentiment. By the supernatural strength of the Holy Spirit, John is calling us to *behold* this groundbreaking gospel truth. This love of God our Father is an incomprehensible reality. It cannot even be revealed to us by flesh and blood. This kind of truth must be winged into the depths of our being by the Word of God and the Spirit of God.

In his letter to the Ephesians, Paul prays for this very thing to occur. Check this out:

> For this reason I kneel before the Father, from whom every family in heaven and on earth derives its name. I pray that out of his glorious riches he may strengthen you with power through his Spirit in your inner being, so that Christ may dwell in your hearts through faith. And I pray that you, being rooted and established in love, may have power, together with all the Lord's holy people, to grasp how wide and long and high and deep is the love of Christ, and to know this love that surpasses knowledge—that you may be filled to the measure of all the fullness of God. (3:14–19)

Paul prays for us to *behold* because the outcome of true beholding is genuine becoming. We become like whom we behold. In this instance, "filled to the measure of all the fullness of God." Would you be willing to dwell in this text for the next several days? Even now, as an act of devotion, would you be willing to copy it down on paper with a pencil or pen?

Linger with the words. Speak them aloud. Paul speaks of a profoundly supernatural activity here.

Let's revisit the end of today's text: "But we know that when he appears we shall be like him, because we shall see him as he is. And everyone who thus hopes in him purifies himself as he is pure" (1 John 3:2–3 ESV).

Did you see the connection? Beholding leads to becoming: "We shall be like him." We cannot "do" our way into being like him. Nor can we "be" our way into being like him. We can behold him and participate in the Holy Spirit's work of making us become like him.

One more for the road today: "Now the Lord is the Spirit, and where the Spirit of the Lord is, there is freedom. And we all, who with unveiled faces [behold] the Lord's glory, are being transformed into his image with ever-increasing glory, which comes from the Lord, who is the Spirit" (2 Cor. 3:17–18).

Pray for the Spirit to make me a beholder today, and I will pray the same for you. This life we seek does not come from accelerated activity. It is the fruit of attentive abandonment to Jesus.

The Prayer

Lord Jesus, teach me this way of beholding; of seeing beyond sight and hearing beyond sound. I will to give you my full and complete attention, but I can only behold by the gift of your Spirit. And I can only become like you by the gift of your Spirit. Lead me in this way. I pray in your name, Jesus. Amen.

The Question

Do you believe it is possible to be "filled to the measure of all the fullness of God" (Eph. 3:19)? How might you behold this fullness? Why are you so distracted?

9 If Sin Has Lost Its Power, How Can It Keep on Winning?

1 JOHN 3:4–6 | **Everyone who sins breaks the law; in fact, sin is lawlessness. But you know that he appeared so that he might take away our sins. And in him is no sin. No one who lives in him keeps on sinning. No one who continues to sin has either seen him or known him.**

Consider This

1. Everyone who sins breaks the law. AGREE.
2. In fact, sin is lawlessness. AGREE.
3. But you know that he appeared so that he might take away our sins. AGREE.
4. And in him is no sin. AGREE.
5. No one who lives in him keeps on sinning. UM . . .
6. No one who continues to sin has either seen him or known him. UH . . .

Agreeing with 1 through 4? Not a problem.

I don't know about you, but I struggle with understanding points 5 and 6. There are only three basic options:

a. It's not true. John heard the Holy Spirit wrong.

b. John means something completely different when he uses the word "sin."

c. It's true.

I choose c. John uses the word *hamartia*, which means to miss the target. Many, many people believe it is impossible to live free from sin. In other words, they believe human beings are destined to miss the mark. I would agree with them if it weren't for Jesus. Because of the work of Jesus on the cross to forgive us of our sin and because of the power of his resurrection to give us power over sin, we can actually hit the target now.

I don't know about you, but I don't want to go through life aiming at a target that I know I will never be able to hit. Do you know what happens to people who believe they can't possibly hit the target? They stop trying to hit it. They resign themselves to miss the mark, which is another way of saying they don't believe sin has lost its power.

What if we began to get focused on actually aiming at the target?

I think the biggest problem Christians have with sin is our lack of belief that it can be overcome. Think of the sin you most struggle to overcome. Do you really want to overcome it? It starts with believing its possible.

The Prayer

Lord Jesus, thank you for showing us what it looks like when a human being hits the target. I confess that becoming like you means learning to hit the target more than I miss it. Come, Holy Spirit, and improve my aim and empower my aspiration. I believe. Help my unbelief. In your name, Jesus. Amen.

The Question

Could it be that we miss the target because our focus is on trying not to miss it? What if our sustained focus were on aiming to hit it? How might the adage "Aim small—miss small" apply in this instance?

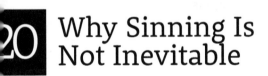 Why Sinning Is Not Inevitable

1 JOHN 3:7–8 | Dear children, do not let anyone lead you astray. The one who does what is right is righteous, just as he is righteous. The one who does what is sinful is of the devil, because the devil has been sinning from the beginning. The reason the Son of God appeared was to destroy the devil's work.

Consider This

I think I'm beginning to understand why John keeps repeating himself when he warns us to not let anyone lead us astray.

I think it must be pretty easy to be led astray. In fact, in light of these texts teaching us it is possible to live free from sin, I think we have all been led astray. We have been led to believe sin is inevitable. The popular bumper sticker says it best: "I'm not perfect, just forgiven." The basic ethic of the Christian when it comes to sin is to be forgiven, be grateful, and do your best to be better.

The one who does what is sinful is of the devil, because the devil has been sinning from the beginning.

I'll be honest: when I sin, my first thought isn't that I am "of the devil." My first thought is that I'm human. Sin is part of being human, right? But what if it's not? What if, in fact, sin actually dehumanizes us? What if being human means not sinning? From the first sin to the most recent one, they all degrade our humanity. Sin makes us less than we were created to be.

Don't hear me wrong. We human beings are sinners, but because of the gospel of Jesus Christ, we have power over sin. We have power to not sin. Sin has lost its power. So, if sin has lost its power, maybe the problem is we have not taken up our power.

What if you got a letter in the mail today with the news that a distant relative had passed away and left you a million dollars? What would you do? You would figure out exactly what you had to do to claim your inheritance, wouldn't you? Imagine just throwing the letter away and forgetting about it.

So, what if you got a letter today with news that you had inherited a power that could enable you to live at a new level of aliveness and creativity and power and love; a power that could free you from selfishness and sadness and addiction and every other way of life that brought grief? What would you do? I can't speak for you, but I would do whatever I needed to do to claim that inheritance.

Here's the good news. John sent you the letter with the news informing that you have inherited power that sets you free from sin—all the ways and patterns of life that rob you and others of life. Are you ready to claim that inheritance? Can you imagine just throwing that letter away and forgetting all about it?

The reason the Son of God appeared was to destroy the devil's work.

Sin has lost its power. Are you ready to take up your inheritance of his power to live the life you were created for?

The Prayer

Lord Jesus, thank you for showing us what it looks like to be a real human being—that it looks like a life that hits the bull's-eye. Would you infuse me with your Spirit in such a way that I live above and beyond the power of sin, which has lost its power? Let me live in the fullness of the freedom of the children of God. Let me claim my inheritance. In your name I pray, Jesus. Amen.

The Question

Are you ready to take the "I'm not perfect, just forgiven" bumper sticker off of your life? What might this mean practically? How might you claim your inheritance?

21 The Orange Juice Concentrate Approach to Faith versus Simply Orange

1 JOHN 3:9–10 | No one who is born of God will continue to sin, because God's seed remains in them; they cannot go on sinning, because they have been born of God. This is how we know who the children of God are and who the children of the devil are: Anyone who does not do what is right is not God's child, nor is anyone who does not love their brother and sister.

Consider This

OK, so I know I am born of God but I continue to sin, yet today's text tells me that if I am born of God, I will not continue to sin. What gives?

If I am honest, I am a living, walking denial of the truth of this text. Either I am not born of God or I am not getting something.

Let's just say I am missing something. Here's how I have been thinking about that.

There are two basic kinds of orange juice: orange juice made from concentrate and orange juice squeezed from oranges. For those of us who didn't grow up with Simply Orange, we made our orange juice from little frozen cans of gooey and strong orange syrup. Mom would thaw the can overnight and dump it into a pitcher the next morning. After running a half gallon of water into the pitcher, she would stir it vigorously. If the juice sat still for any length of time, the concentrate would settle to the bottom. It always had to be shaken up again. In retrospect, I suppose it was the next best thing to Tang.

This is a good analogy for our life of faith. I think when most of us became Christians we got a good dose of the pure concentrate, but over time we have diluted it down over and over again with more and more water. It hardly tastes like anything anymore. Oh, we've been shaken up a number of times over the years, and the taste will get stronger for a while, but over time it's lost its punch.

Then there's the other kind of orange juice; the stuff like Simply Orange. Remember when that came on the market? The taste does not compare, nor does the price. Whenever I buy orange juice, I'm looking for those three magic words on the label: NOT FROM CONCENTRATE. That's another way of saying "the real thing."

I can't speak for you, but I think my problem is I've settled for a little "Jesus concentrate" and slowly but surely, it's gotten watered down and lost its punch. I'm tired of watered-down. I want the "not from concentrate" Christian faith. I want "Simply Jesus."

John is giving us a good shake with today's text:

This is how we know who the children of God are and who the children of the devil are: Anyone who does not do what is right is not God's child, nor is anyone who does not love their brother and sister.

A good shaking up, however, will never get it done. What we need is the not-from-concentrate, Simply Jesus stuff. How do we get it? First, we've got to be sick and tired of the watered-down variety. That's called holy discontent. Then we need to ask the Holy Spirit to lead us into this Simply Jesus way, the new not-from-concentrate way of belonging to God.

The Prayer

Lord Jesus, you are the real thing. I want my life to be the real thing. I am tired of a watered-down version of faith. I want Simply Jesus. Give me the courage to name my discontent with where I am. Save me from the trap of shaming myself over my discontent. Let the truth set me free to live at a new level with you. Take me to a new place of life in you. I pray in your name, Jesus. Amen.

The Question

How do you relate to this orange juice concentrate metaphor for our relationship with Jesus versus a "not from concentrate" kind of relationship? What might a step toward making the switch look like?

22 The Powerful Principle of Displacement

1 JOHN 3:11 KJ21 | For this is the message that ye heard from the beginning: that we should love one another.

Consider This

If First John can be said to be about anything, it can be said to be about first things.

That which was from the beginning . . . (1 John 1:1)

This is the message we have heard from him and declare to you: God is light; in him there is no darkness at all. (1 John 1:5)

Dear friends, I am not writing you a new command but an old command that you have had from the beginning. The old command is the message you have heard. (1 John 2:7 HCSB)

As for you, see that what you have heard from the beginning remains in you. (1 John 2:24)

For this is the message that ye heard from the beginning . . .
Light or darkness, God or Satan, love or hate. John has to be one of the most straightforward teachers of the New Testament. He does it in the same way that all great leaders do it, through drawing contrast. It's this not that.

We gain our understanding of darkness in the light of Light; of Satan by the presence of God; of hate through the movement of love. In the process we learn perhaps the most important lesson of all: the principle of displacement. This is not a fair fight. These are not well-matched opponents. Light need only show up—darkness disappears. God need only come on the scene—Satan flees. In the same way light displaces darkness and God displaces Satan, love displaces sin.

We should love one another.

I've said it here before. I'll say it again. Love is not soft. It is the most hardcore power in the universe. Love is not the mushy sentiment it's made out to be, nor is it the passionate feeling we so often want it to be. Love is the Jesus-inspired, Holy Spirit–fueled, will-of-God-powered way of life that always puts others before ourselves. Love creates life. Love overcomes the impossible. Signs and wonders are merely the tipping point of divine love in the midst of human community. Love is not a truce that gets passed off as peace. Neither is it some dysfunctional compromise that gets passed off as unity.

I will go so far as to say that love is the only creative power in the world. Every other so-called power is a counterfeit power claiming rogue authority, and its ultimate contribution to the world is not creativity but more chaos. In the end, love will be the blinding, merciful light of the pierced and piercing justice of God, in whose presence anything less simply cannot remain. It's why in the end we must be made like him, else we be made nothing.

Love is the preexistent reality of Father-Son-Holy Spirit. Love was the preeminent reality in the creation of all that is. Love was the first thing and it will be the last thing, and in the end it will be the only thing. Love is the glory of God.

We should love one another.

Jesus could not have been more clear. He said people would know we were his followers by the way we loved one another (John 13:35).

The task we have is that of getting crystal-clear clarity about the meaning of this term that has been bandied about so much that it means nothing anymore. That's where John is headed. Hold on!

The Prayer

Lord Jesus, you are the Lamb of God, who takes away the sin of the world. You are the Light of the world, who takes away the darkness. You are the love of God that overcomes our sin. Shift my gravity from all my efforts against darkness and Satan and sin into the irresistible, compelling gravity of light and the Spirit and love. Teach me this way of holy displacement. I pray in your name, Jesus. Amen.

The Question

What would it take for love to actually become the controlling power of your life? How might the principle of displacement work in your life?

23 | "I'm a Mac, and I'm a PC": How the Great Leaders Lead Change

1 JOHN 3:12–13 | Do not be like Cain, who belonged to the evil one and murdered his brother. And why did he murder him? Because his own actions were evil and his brother's were righteous. Do not be surprised, my brothers and sisters, if the world hates you.

Consider This

Remember the famous "Get a Mac" series of television commercials, with the two contrasting characters? Most of the ads began with the familiar, "I'm a Mac." "And I'm a PC." (Google "I'm a Mac" videos and you will find them.) These advertisements weren't about computers. They were about the people who use computers. They weren't showing us which computer we should buy as much as they were showing us who we wanted to become—the Mac guy, not the PC guy.

Great leaders lead with a vision that inspires us to become more than we are.

So often Christian leaders focus us more on who we don't want to be or what we shouldn't be doing or how we should try harder to *not* do this or that. The great leaders of the Christian movement cast a vision of who God wants us to become. They don't so much get in our faces as they grab ahold of our hearts. Sure, they deal with sin, but only as a contrast device. The real game is in the vision of becoming.

That's what's going on in today's text. "I'm Cain." "And I'm Abel." Cain belonged to Satan. Abel loved God. Cain murdered Abel. Bad Cain. This visionary use of contrast proceeds literally through the whole Bible. There's Noah and then there's everybody else. How about Abraham and Lot, or Moses and Pharaoh? Then there's Elijah and the prophets of Baal, and King Saul and King David. How about Jesus contrasting the types of soil or the house built on the rock versus on the sand? On we could go. The Bible constantly calls us to *this*, not *that*. It's all about becoming.

It's just so critical that we have a "be like this" mind-set and not just a "don't do that." Would you rather someone tell you to aim at the bull's-eye, or "Don't miss"? That's exactly where John is headed. He is calling us to aim at a very particular variety of love; to aspire to a way of life—eternal life—here and now. Eternal life is life on another level. It's life in the light of love. It will come down to Jesus, not Satan, and to the kingdom, not the world.

So how about you? Mac or PC?

The Prayer

Lord Jesus, you are the way and the truth and the life. I want to know you, to behold you, and to become like you. You are the bull's-eye of the target at which I am aiming my life. Shift my focus from not losing to actually winning. Not only are you the way; you are the Way Maker. I pray in your name, Jesus. Amen.

The Question

It is easy to live with a vague sense of aspiring to be like Jesus. How can this become more positively specific? How can you move from an ethereal, general idea of hitting the target to something far more specific? In what particular way is the Holy Spirit leading you to become like Jesus? How can you get your aim on that?

24 | Are You Saved? Are You Sure? How Do You Know?

1 JOHN 3:14–15 | We know that we have passed from death to life, because we love each other. Anyone who does not love remains in death. Anyone who hates a brother or sister is a murderer, and you know that no murderer has eternal life residing in him.

Consider This

How does a person know he or she has crossed over from darkness and entered into life or that he or she has been delivered from death to life?

Is the old hymn lyric accurate: "You ask me how I know he lives / He lives within my heart"?

According to John, those lyrics should look more like, "You ask me how I know he lives / I know because I actually love people now."

In all seriousness, people want assurance that their eternal salvation is secured. Many come at this by declaring it as a type of fiat, claiming texts such as Romans 10:9: "If you confess with your mouth, 'Jesus is Lord,' and believe in your heart that God raised Him from the dead, you will be saved" (HCSB).

Others come at the notion of the security of one's salvation through a route of inward assurance from the Holy Spirit. They cite texts such as Romans 8:16: "The Spirit himself bears witness with our spirit that we are children of God" (ESV).

So, on the one hand there's the evidence of the "confession" outlined by Romans 10:9, and on the other there's the more subjective evidence of the inner witness referenced in Romans 8:16. John has a different kind of evidence altogether.

We know that we have passed from death to life, because we love each other.

Note the implicit claim within the statement. Because of sin, the default position for all people is death. Salvation means passing from death to life. Note that John is not claiming that one passes from death to life *because of* his or her love for others. He says we can be *assured* we have passed from death to life because we love each other. In other words, loving one another is not the condition for salvation but the evidence of it. In Ephesians 2:8–9, Scripture makes it plain that nothing we can do earns our salvation: "For it is by grace you have been saved, through faith—and this is not from yourselves, it is the gift of God—not by works, so that no one can boast."

In John's gospel we see something that remarkably resembles today's text: "Very truly I tell you, whoever hears my word and believes him who sent me has eternal life and will not be judged but has crossed over from death to life" (John 5:24). For John, the assurance of one's salvation or the quality of one's eternal security is not assessed by the appropriateness of his or her confession of faith, nor can it be determined by his or her inner experience of the Holy Spirit. It can only be known by the inward bearing and outward behavior of one person toward another.

Real love is not just right actions. Paul makes it clear that a person can demonstrate nothing short of what appears to be heroic benevolence toward other people and still be bereft of real love. He deems this kind of activity as worthless. (See 1 Corinthians 13.) On the other hand, an inner feeling toward others that finds no outward expression can't be considered real love either.

So maybe the question is not so much, How is it with your soul? but rather, How is it with your relationships? What if the more accurate barometer of faith is not some existential sense of inner peace but rather the shared experience of the peace of Christ in our relationships?

John's going to get even more focused and specific in the coming days. Stay with me. First John may be all at once the most theological and most practical book in the entire Bible.

The Prayer

Lord Jesus, you are the love of God, and it is only your presence in our relationships that can release the love of God among us. You taught us to love one another as you loved us. You taught us that the only way people will know we follow you is by the way we love one another. Wake us up to this truth. Give us the courage to become graciously honest with ourselves about our relationships with others and what that tells us about our relationship with you. We pray in your name, Jesus. Amen.

The Question

So how is it with your relationships? And what does that tell you about your real relationship with Jesus? Are you uncomfortable with this line of questioning?

5 Why the Rest of the Gospel Is the Best of the Gospel

1 JOHN 3:16 | This is how we know what love is: Jesus Christ laid down his life for us. And we ought to lay down our lives for our brothers and sisters.

Consider This

The most popular verse in the Bible without a doubt is John 3:16. In case you need reminding, here it is: "For God so loved the world that He gave His only begotten Son, that whosoever believeth in Him should not perish, but have everlasting life" (kj21).

This verse is clearly the banner and battle cry for what I call the first half of the gospel. By that I mean the initial decision to trust Jesus by confession, repentance, and baptism.

I am on a campaign to make 1 John 3:16 the banner verse and battle cry of the second half of the gospel, or the rest of the gospel, as I like to say it. By that I mean the ongoing process of abandoning one's life to Jesus Christ in love for the sake of others coming to know him. It is the movement from *believing* the love of God in Jesus Christ to *becoming* the love of God in Jesus Christ. It's why I also like to say, "The rest of the gospel is the best of the gospel."

This is how we know what love is: Jesus Christ laid down his life for us. And we ought to lay down our lives for our brothers and sisters.

So why this text as the banner for the second half of the gospel? Because it clearly and simply and profoundly defines what God means by love. Why do we need that? Here's an example of how the dictionary might define love:

love: (1) a feeling of strong or constant affection for a person. (2) attraction that includes sexual desire: the strong affection felt by people who have a romantic relationship. (3) the object of attachment, devotion, or admiration.

The world's translation of today's text would look like this:

> This is how we know what love is: a feeling of strong or constant affection, attraction, or sexual desire for a person.

Now compare again with the Bible's definition:

> This is how we know what love is: Jesus Christ laid down his life for us. And we ought to lay down our lives for our brothers and sisters.

I'm not knocking feelings of strong or constant affection or attraction or romance. I'm just saying for the sake of clarity that we should probably just refer to that as feelings of strong or constant affection or attraction or romance rather than calling it love.

Nothing is more beautiful or winsome or powerful than people laying down their interests and agendas and needs and desires for the best interests of others. In fact, the most descriptive word for this kind of love is *holy*. It's why at Seedbed we often pair the words together to distinguish the kind of love for which we want to raise a banner: holy love.

How about it? Will you join the campaign? First John 3:16. I'm loading it into my "rememberizer" today. Let's raise a banner.

This is how we know what love is: Jesus Christ laid down his life for us. And we ought to lay down our lives for our brothers and sisters.

The Prayer

Lord Jesus, you laid down your life for us, and you were gloriously raised from the dead. You call us to follow you in this way of the cross. Why is this so hard for us? Reveal to me what keeps me so stuck in my own self-interest. Break me free to live freely as one who gives without measure or calculation. Take me to a place of death to myself that I might be raised to a life of more aliveness to others. In your name I pray, Jesus. Amen.

The Question

Are you ready to start moving at a new pace into the second half of the gospel? Are you ready to share this journey with someone else? Remember, we can't learn to walk this way alone. Reread 1 John 3:16. What holds you back? Will it be worth it later if you don't make this move in your life?

26 People Need Help, Not Pity

1 JOHN 3:17–18 | If anyone has material possessions and sees a brother or sister in need but has no pity on them, how can the love of God be in that person? Dear children, let us not love with words or speech but with actions and in truth.

Consider This

Remember that time Jesus said this:

> "Then he will say to those on his left, 'Depart from me, you who are cursed, into the eternal fire prepared for the devil and his angels. For I was hungry and you gave me nothing to eat, I was thirsty and you gave me nothing to drink, I was a stranger and you did not invite me in, I needed clothes and you did not clothe me, I was sick and in prison and you did not look after me.'
>
> "They also will answer, 'Lord, when did we see you hungry or thirsty or a stranger or needing clothes or sick or in prison, and did not help you?'
>
> "He will reply, 'Truly I tell you, whatever you did not do for one of the least of these, you did not do for me.'
>
> "Then they will go away to eternal punishment, but the righteous to eternal life." (Matt. 25:41–46)

Yeah, that's what John is saying in today's text:

> If anyone has material possessions and sees a brother or sister in need but has no pity on them, how can the love of God be in that person?

Now, let's remember our banner verse from yesterday, 1 John 3:16:

> This is how we know what love is: Jesus Christ laid down his life for us. And we ought to lay down our lives for our brothers and sisters.

In case we were thinking John was talking about martyrdom, he shows us that "to lay down our lives for our brothers and sisters" can be as simple as sharing with another person in need.

Now, let me point out something I find very interesting about this phrase "has no pity on them." I don't know about you, but I've never had a positive feeling about pity. In my understanding, pity means to feel sorry for someone. People who need help don't typically want you to feel sorry for them. They want you to help them. Who wants pity?

When I dug into the text, I learned that the Greek word, *kleise*, behind the phrase "has no pity on them" actually means "to close up one's heart." To close my heart to a person in need strikes me as something altogether different from having no pity on that person.

Further, helping someone in need is not about giving someone some spare change. It's not an obligatory act. The holy love of God is about compassion, which is a Holy Spirit–inspired disposition of the heart that leads to action. The big issue isn't whether we are helping people in need; it's whether our hearts are truly open to those we are helping. I've helped people in need many times just to make myself feel better, but I can't say my heart was truly open to them. Know what I mean?

Dear children, let us not love with words or speech but with actions and in truth.

That's it! Love means doing something for another from the deep wellsprings of Christ in us. It's not just actions, nor is it mere truth. Love is a holy compulsion to help others, everywhere, all the time, no matter what . . . so help us God.

John isn't trying to shake us up. He's shaking us down. He's not accusing us but awakening us. This is not about already being there. It's all about being on the way. According to Jesus, there's a lot at stake here. Let's not be afraid of asking ourselves the hard questions. Only the truth will set us free.

The Prayer

Lord Jesus, you know I want to help others and you know what a challenge it is every time I see a person in need. In the face of overwhelming need and intractable challenges, give me the courage to love with action. Teach my heart to follow my help. I can't do it without you. I pray in your name. Amen.

The Question

Have you ever given help with a closed heart? What would it look like to open your heart to people in need?

7 Why You Shouldn't Trust Your Conscience

1 JOHN 3:19–20 HCSB | **This is how we will know we belong to the truth and will convince our conscience in His presence, even if our conscience condemns us, that God is greater than our conscience, and He knows all things.**

Consider This

Let your conscience be your guide. We hear stuff like that all the time. People readily equate the work of the Holy Spirit with one's conscience. It's not so. Just as John began his sermon dealing with the deception of the self-assured people who claimed to have no sin, now he turns to another group of potentially self-deceived folks on the other side of the fence. In today's text, John addresses those whose consciences may be deceiving them.

Consider this hypothetical situation: the preacher at First Sinners Church preaches a sermon in which he strongly confronts the congregation on their lack of care for people in need. Most of the congregants have one of two very different responses. One group agrees with the preacher's assessment and immediately heaps shame on themselves for their failure. The other group rises up in pride-filled indignation that the preacher would say such a thing to them. Group #1, the self-shamers, feel as though they should have done more. They slink downward in a type of self-condemnation that masquerades as their individual consciences. Group #2, the self-justifiers, rise up in stiff-necked self-defense.

What I want us to notice is that the responses of group #1 and group #2 are really the same; they are two sides of the same coin. Both revolve around a self-oriented way of thinking: self-abnegation on the one hand and self-assuredness on the other. Each has a completely different yet totally related way of dealing with the issue. The shame people think they are bad. The pride people think they are good.

The massively glaring problem is no one is actually thinking about people in need because they are completely self-absorbed in thinking about themselves. It's why we should trust neither our confidence nor our consciences. John exhorts us to examine the evidence. Just because a person feels as if he has cancer doesn't mean he has cancer. There's a simple way to find out. It's called a biopsy. Just because a person feels she has a healthy heart doesn't mean she has a healthy heart. There's a simple way to find out. It's called a stress test. *This is how we will know we belong to the truth and will convince our conscience in His presence, even if our conscience condemns . . .* So what is the "this"? It's actually the previous "this," from verse 16, which is better explained in verse 18:

> This is how we know what love is: Jesus Christ laid down his life for us. And we ought to lay down our lives for our brothers and sisters. . . . Dear children, let us not love with words or speech but with actions and in truth.

We know we belong to the truth if our love is characterized by the inside-out dynamic of truth. Truth is ever asking the question, Is our inward reality of love becoming the outward activity of love? If it is not, then we can question whether we belong to the truth. It's not a question of how much is enough. That's the misleading math of the conscience. We can always do more. The issue isn't quantity of activity but quality of activity. If we are measuring quantity, it's usually about what we've done. If we are measuring quality, it's more about who we've helped. Both now and in the end, we can trust God. As John closes today's text: *God is greater than our conscience, and He knows all things.* Bottom line: be honest with yourself. Do your best to love others. Trust God with the rest.

The Prayer

Lord Jesus, save me from the twin traps of self-justification and self-abnegation. Set me free from these false selves that I might become able to give myself away. Thank you for showing us what love is. Make that manifest through my life to others. I pray in your name. Amen.

The Question

Do you tend to be a self-shamer or self-justifier? How will you move off of this continuum or plane of existence? What will it take?

28 How Condemnation Works and Why It Loses

1 JOHN 3:21–22 ESV | Beloved, if our heart does not condemn us, we have confidence before God; and whatever we ask we receive from him, because we keep his commandments and do what pleases him.

Consider This

I don't know about you, but there have been times in my life when I have committed sin, received forgiveness, done it again, asked forgiveness again, and again, until finally I reached a point where I felt a terrible sense of condemnation. I naturally feel this condemnation is coming from God, when in truth it's probably coming more from my own sense of guilt and shame. Bottom line: I have no confidence in bringing this before God any longer.

Some of you may be thinking, *Of course God condemns sinful behavior, especially when repeated over and over again.* I would point you to Romans 7, which highlights the condition of repeatedly doing that which you hate. The deeper truth comes in Romans 8:1: "There is therefore now no condemnation for those who are in Christ Jesus" (ESV).

John told us earlier that we must abandon our self-abnegation and return to confession, no matter how many times it takes. Remember this from 1 John 1:9: "If we confess our sins, he is faithful and just and will forgive us our sins and purify us from all unrighteousness"?

We can experience defeat without actually being defeated. Condemnation is a satanic strategy designed to lead us deeper into defeat, keeping us away from the only One who can heal us.

This path of persistent confession is the only pathway by which we are set free of the condemnation we heap on ourselves. We must keep returning as many times as it takes. If Jesus tells us to forgive a person seventy times seven, how much more do you think he will forgive us? This gospel of mercy and grace empowers us to come before God with confidence and even boldness. This is not taking a casual approach to grace. It's actually a quite serious approach to sin. Satan wants us to disqualify ourselves from grace, which can only lead to more and more sin and death. Jesus tells us that because grace will not let us go, we must never let go of grace. The only way through sin is a deeper and more doggedly determined engagement of grace.

Beloved, if our heart does not condemn us, we have confidence before God; and whatever we ask we receive from him, because we keep his commandments and do what pleases him.

So, what's this bit about receiving from God anything we ask? It's a mistake to read this text as an if-then (i.e., if we behave, God will bless). This is all about persevering in a relationship with God until the Word and ways and will of God break through in our lives. This is life in the zone of abiding. This is a fruit of real discipleship. It's coming to a place with God that is a pure gift though we had to contend and wrestle to get there. This is the place Jesus described when he spoke of asking and receiving, seeking and finding, and knocking and the door opening.

Let's give Jesus the last word today with two quotes from John's gospel:

And I will do whatever you ask in my name, so that the Father may be glorified in the Son. You may ask me for anything in my name, and I will do it. (John 14:13–14)

> If you remain in me and my words remain in you,
> ask whatever you wish, and it will be done for you.
> (John 15:7)

The Prayer

Lord Jesus, thank you for this really good news about there being no condemnation for your followers, no matter what. Teach me this way of taking sin seriously yet taking grace more seriously. Come, Holy Spirit, and give me perseverance in this war of grace until sin is defeated and I am free. In your name, Jesus. Amen.

The Question

Is there a persistent, even besetting sin that will not stop in your life? Have you given up on fighting it? Will you rise again and renew your confession before God and not give up until grace wins? How about now?

9 The Difference between Certainty and Clarity

1 JOHN 3:23–24 | And this is his command: to believe in the name of his Son, Jesus Christ, and to love one another as he commanded us. The one who keeps God's commands lives in him, and he in them. And this is how we know that he lives in us: We know it by the Spirit he gave us.

Consider This

Today's text brings us another recurrence of the "this is," phrase followed by a declarative definition. Clearly, John is working in a context of confusion. False teaching can be devastating to people. Ideas have consequences. Theological ideas take consequences to the next level. It's very tempting to take a posture of "think and let think" when it comes to divergent takes on biblical and theological truth. It's actually quite devastating. John aims for basic, gut-level clarity. It's worth revisiting the (at least) seven previous occurrences of the "this is" phrase before going forward. The montage follows:

> That which was from the beginning, which we have heard, which we have seen with our eyes, which we have looked at and our hands have touched—*this [is what] we proclaim* concerning the Word of life. (1:1)

> *This is the message* we have heard from him and proclaim to you, that God is light, and in him is no darkness at all. (1:5 ESV)

> *This is how we know* who the children of God are and who the children of the devil are: Anyone who does not do what is right is not God's child, nor is anyone who does not love their brother and sister. (3:10)

> *For this is the message* you have heard from the beginning: We should love one another. (3:11 HCSB)

This is how we know what love is: Jesus Christ laid down his life for us. And we ought to lay down our lives for our brothers and our sisters. (3:16)

This is how we will know we belong to the truth and will convince our conscience in His presence, even if our conscience condemns us, that God is greater than our conscience, and He knows all things. (3:19–20 HCSB)

Now *this is His command*: that we believe in the name of His Son Jesus Christ, and love one another as He commanded us. (3:23 HCSB)

And *this is how we know* that he lives in us. We know it by the Spirit that he gave us. (3:24)

So often, people crave certainty when it comes to faith, just as they did in Paul's time. Something about faith and certainty don't seem to go together. Certainty counterfeits faith and produces an appealing but powerless dogmatism. Clarity, on the other hand, flowers into faith and leads to the fruitful and often vulnerable obedience of love. In my judgment, it is far more important to have clarity than certainty. Certainty produces a type of self-confidence in leaders that can be very appealing in times of uncertainty and confusion. Clarity creates the conditions, not for self-confidence, but for courageous faith.

False teaching bullies people with its confident certainty. The truth patiently and persistently labors for courageous clarity. The Spirit is always on the side of clarity.

The Prayer

Lord Jesus, thank you for making the gospel so clear. Thank you for showing me how I can know what love is and how I can know I belong to the truth and how I can know that you live in me. Save me from the temptation of seeking an easy certainty when you are calling for courageous faith. Teach me to cling to your clarity and so become a clear witness to others. In your name I pray. Amen.

The Question

Where in your faith do you need more clarity? Is your confidence in Jesus rooted more in your self-generated certainty or in Jesus' clear teaching and example?

30 Put Your Leaders to the Test

1 JOHN 4:1–3 HCSB | Dear friends, do not believe every spirit, but test the spirits to determine if they are from God, because many false prophets have gone out into the world.

This is how you know the Spirit of God: Every spirit who confesses that Jesus Christ has come in the flesh is from God. But every spirit who does not confess Jesus is not from God. This is the spirit of the antichrist; you have heard that he is coming, and he is already in the world now.

Consider This

If there's one thing we can say about a false prophet, it's that he doesn't wear a T-shirt that says "false prophet." In other words, false prophets can be very difficult to spot. A bogus prophet or a deceptive teacher often presents a slightly gray-shaded version of the truth, rather than a glaring error anyone can spot. False prophets often come across with a strong sense of authority. In fact, their teaching can seem so reasonable and even compelling that it seems they carry the anointing of the Holy Spirit.

It's why John warns us to "test the spirits." Note that he's *not* telling us to trust our guts or our instincts or our sense of discernment or what other authorities we trust may or may not say. John gives us a far more objective criterion.

This is how you know the Spirit of God: Every spirit who confesses that Jesus Christ has come in the flesh is from God. But every spirit who does not confess Jesus is not from God.

It all comes back to Jesus. Jesus is *the* Truth. If we do not comprehend and confess the truth about *the* Truth, we are sitting ducks for false teachers. Hear me straight here. This is not about saying the right words or saying the words right. False teachers play fast and loose with the meaning of words. False teaching, or heresy, always comes back to a distortion of the truth about Jesus.

Some months ago, I was in a church where a noted Jewish New Testament scholar was invited to teach. She was brilliant and compelling and exceedingly coherent in her teaching. She had given her life to the study of Jesus of Nazareth. She is one of the foremost authorities on Jesus and the New Testament on the planet.

After her message, the pastor graciously opened the floor for questions. The people, very generous in their response, marveled at her interpretations of certain passages of Scripture they had never understood before. It amazed me just how ready they were to completely buy her message and get on board with her program.

I sensed the Holy Spirit moving me to ask a question, and not just any question, but THE question. I didn't want to do it, but I was compelled to raise my hand. When the microphone came my way, I stood, and in as kind and gracious a manner as I could, I posed this question: "Do you believe God raised Jesus Christ from the dead?"

She answered, "No."

In my lawyerly mind I thought to myself, *No further questions*, and I sat down.

I respect her for her honesty. I admire her devotion to the study of the New Testament. I am certain I could learn many true things from her about Jesus of Nazareth. But as far as I'm concerned, no matter how much she knows about the New Testament, her inability to confess Jesus Christ as risen from the dead effectively disqualifies her as a teacher of the church. While I'm certain she is not a charlatan or a dishonest person, I do believe she is a false teacher.

John, in essence, tells us that when it comes to false teachers, don't walk; run. When it comes to Jesus Christ, we cannot have a "think and let think" mentality. When the central truth of the gospel is even a shade off center, the circumference of the message will be cloaked in shadows and the consequences will be catastrophic.

It's why we literally need to put our would-be leaders on the proverbial witness stand and kindly, graciously, with the love of God, ask them what they believe about Jesus. Something like this:

> Do you believe in the Lord Jesus Christ, the only begotten Son of God . . . God of God, Light of light, very God of very God, begotten, not made, of one substance with the Father, by whom all things were made? Do you believe he was born of the Virgin Mary? Suffered under Pontius Pilate? Was crucified, dead, and buried? Do you believe that on the third day he arose from the dead? Ascended into heaven? And sits at the right hand of God the Father Almighty? Do you believe from there he will come to judge the living and the dead?

And after this, we must press in further and make certain of what they mean when they say he was raised from the dead. Was this a spiritual resurrection or a bodily resurrection? Is this a metaphor or a historical fact?

This is how we test the spirits. I don't want to bully anyone with a strong-armed sense of certainty, but I make no apology for an overabundance of clarity on these matters. Something tells me John would agree.

The Prayer

Lord Jesus, thank you for the clarity of your life. And thank you for insisting that we be clear about it. Grant us the discernment of the Holy Spirit to "test the spirits" and the courage to run from false teaching and teachers. We pray in your name, Jesus. Amen.

The Question

Are you clear on the central and core truths concerning our Lord, Jesus Christ? Are your present leaders and teachers clear on this? How might you graciously discern this?

31 What in the World Is the World?

1 JOHN 4:4–6 ESV | Little children, you are from God and have overcome them, for he who is in you is greater than he who is in the world. They are from the world; therefore they speak from the world, and the world listens to them. We are from God. Whoever knows God listens to us; whoever is not from God does not listen to us. By this we know the Spirit of truth and the spirit of error.

Consider This

What in the world is "the world"? Is it the planet? Is it Las Vegas? Is it riches and fame? Is it a group of people? Is it the devil? Is it the mall? Is it the ghetto in the inner city? Or is the world the opulent wealth of the suburbs? Is it R-rated movies?

Is the world a bad place? Or is the world the same place that John spoke of when he said, "For God so loved the world that He gave His only begotten Son, that whosoever believeth in Him should not perish, but have everlasting life" (John 3:16 KJ21)?

What in the world is the world, and where is it?

I think I have always thought I knew, but now that I ask the question, I am not so sure.

Though it be filled with evil, the world cannot be a bad place. I think the issue isn't so much the world as it is the one who is in the world. The world, to be sure, is a fallen place. Because of the one who is in the world, the world lives in the throes of a conspiracy of corruption. The world is love turned into lust. It is beauty reduced to brokenness. The world is home turned into hell. The world is the created supplanting the Creator. The world is the truth exchanged for a lie.

There's a common myth among many Christians that has persisted through the ages to the present day. The myth is that the world is not our home, that we can somehow escape the world or at least boycott it.

But think about it: Jesus didn't teach us to pray, "Thy will be done, somewhere other than here, as it is in heaven." No! It's on earth, right here, in the world, as it is in heaven. (See Matthew 6:9–12.)

The big problem is not that we are in the world. The problem is the world is in us. That's why today's text is such good news.

Little children, you are from God and have overcome them, for he who is in you is greater than he who is in the world. The kingdom comes when this reality is given birth right square in the middle of the real world.

Because of Jesus and the gift of the Holy Spirit, we can live in the world without the world living in us. I like the way Peter puts it:

> His divine power has given us everything we need for a godly life through our knowledge of him who called us by his own glory and goodness. Through these he has given us his very great and precious promises, so that through them you may participate in the divine nature, having escaped the corruption in the world caused by evil desires. (2 Pet. 1:3–4)

We can't escape the world, but we can escape the corruption that is in the world. The secret is the One who is in us.

So how about it? Do you have the viewpoint of the world, or is your vision fixed on Jesus?

The Prayer

Lord Jesus, thank you for the world you created and thank you for graciously recreating it day by day. Thank you for showing us a way not to withdraw from the world but to escape the corruption that is in the world. Come, Holy Spirit, and empower this more and more in us. It's in your name, Jesus, we pray. Amen.

The Question

Do you have a generally negative attitude toward the world? How might you shift your mentality from withdrawing from the chaos and complexities of the world to engaging them? How do you escape the corruption in the midst of it?

32 For the Love of a Hundred-Dollar Bill

1 JOHN 4:7–12 | Dear friends, let us love one another, for love comes from God. Everyone who loves has been born of God and knows God. Whoever does not love does not know God, because God is love. This is how God showed his love among us: He sent his one and only Son into the world that we might live through him. This is love: not that we loved God, but that he loved us and sent his Son as an atoning sacrifice for our sins. Dear friends, since God so loved us, we also ought to love one another. No one has ever seen God; but if we love one another, God lives in us and his love is made complete in us.

Consider This

As I have noted multiple times before, love is not a fleeting feeling but a forceful fact. John said earlier, "This is how we know what love is: Jesus Christ laid down his life for us. And we ought to lay down our lives for our brothers and sisters" (1 John 3:16). Today John says it in yet another way:

> This is love: not that we loved God, but that he loved us and sent his Son as an atoning sacrifice for our sins. Dear friends, since God so loved us, we also ought to love one another.

I have a close friend named Paul who usually carries several hundred dollars in his pocket. One day when we were together, he quietly slipped me a one-hundred-dollar bill. *Wow! What a great gift!* I thought to myself as I embraced and thanked him. I could tell it gave him joy to give it to me.

Within minutes, I found myself talking to one of my friends who I knew struggled weekly to make ends meet. Something in me rose up and inspired me to quietly slip that hundred-dollar bill to my friend. He thanked me profusely and embraced me. I could tell this was hitting him at a really good time. I felt elation within as I walked away from that encounter.

Not only that, but when I told Paul about what I did with the hundred dollars, it made him glad all over again, and I found myself glad about his gladness. Paul gave the money to me out of his love for me. I gave the money to my friend out of love for him. And in freely giving the love Paul had given me to my friend, the love of Paul was mysteriously made complete in me.

No one has ever seen God; but if we love one another, God lives in us and his love is made complete in us.

Love is most fully experienced when the gladness of the giver meets the gratitude of the recipient. Love is made complete when the gladness of the giver gets expressed through the generosity of the recipient to release the gift forward to yet another.

If I'm starting to sound circular in my argument, it's because love is, in fact, circular. But love is not a circle. Love's movement is circular, yet the circle never closes itself but continually expands in an outwardly spiraling movement. I call it "spirilical." Love is the ordinary yet supernatural expression of the ever-expanding, outward-moving spirilical of self-giving generosity.

"No one has ever seen God" . . . but every time this kind of self-giving generosity emerges in the world, God is made manifest.

This is how God showed his love among us: He sent his one and only Son into the world that we might live through him.

Living "through him" is the miracle of the gospel. It means we become "originals," points of origin, places where the love of God is originated.

I think we're onto something.

The Prayer

Lord Jesus, you are truly the original. You are original love, and you are ever ready to originate your love in and through us. Would you nudge me out of my safe self-comfort zone and into a place of originating love for others? I want you to live your life of profound love in and through me for others. I pray in your name, Jesus. Amen.

The Question

What would it mean for your life to become an originating source of the love of Jesus for others? How would this look different than life looks right now? What will be a step in that direction?

33 The Pathways to Progress in Faith

1 JOHN 4:13–16 HCSB | This is how we know that we remain in Him and He in us: He has given assurance to us from His Spirit. And we have seen and we testify that the Father has sent His Son as the world's Savior. Whoever confesses that Jesus is the Son of God—God remains in him and he in God. And we have come to know and to believe the love that God has for us. God is love, and the one who remains in love remains in God, and God remains in him.

Consider This

The Christian life is like a stool supported by three legs. There's the historical witness—external and objective: *And we have seen and testify that the Father has sent His Son as the world's Savior.*

There's the witness of the Spirit—the internal and subjective experience of the objective reality: *This is how we know that we remain in Him and He in us: He has given assurance to us from His Spirit.*

There's the witness of the community—interpersonal and relational: *God is love, and the one who remains in love remains in God, and God remains in him.*

Faith is the crisis of belief, which leads to the process of experience, which becomes the demonstration of the truth in love.

Bringing it home, where are you strong and where do you need to grow?

EMPIRICALLY: Do you struggle to fully embrace the orthodox teaching of the love of God in Jesus Christ? If so, I encourage you to develop a daily practice of affirming the historic creeds of the church. Start with the Apostles' Creed.[4] Just try saying it aloud every morning for the next twenty-eight days. I might also recommend a seven-week daily reflection guide I put together on the Apostles' Creed, titled simply *CREED*. We have a lot of resources along these lines at Seedbed.com.

EXPERIENTIALLY: Do you struggle with the inner experience of the love of God in Jesus Christ? If so, I encourage you to grow in your practice of the means of grace,[5] Scripture (including the daily text); prayer[6] (make it defined through posture, voice, time; clear through writing, etc.); fasting (which takes prayer to the next level of experience);

---

4. A copy of it can be seen at http://www.seedbed.com/apostles-creed/.
5. See Robert J. Stamps, *Jesus & the Means of Grace*, available at http://store.seedbed.com/products/jesus-and-the-means-of-grace.
6. I recommend Winfield Bevins's *Field Guide for Daily Prayer*, available at http://store.seedbed.com/products/field-guide-for-daily-prayer.

conferencing (processing experience with other believers),[7] and Communion (stop trying to understand it and instead posture yourself to behold the mystery of the Lord's Supper).

EXPERIMENTALLY: Do you struggle with the interpersonal expression or demonstration of the love of God in Jesus Christ? If so, I encourage you to grow in your focused intention. Literally construct experiments whereby you do small (and even hidden) acts of loving service to other people. Maxie Dunnam has authored a brilliant study along these lines.[8]

In summary, faith is the mysterious convergence of crisis and process and demonstration built on three corresponding kinds of evidence: empirical, experiential, and experimental.

All of this is, of course, an artificial construct rather than a formula. We need handles on faith in order to grow in our discipleship. It doesn't just happen. Let's get on with the second half of the gospel—that's where the action is. Let this time be a new season to freshly consecrate yourself to Jesus in some tangible ways.

---

7. A good resource on this is *The Class Meeting: Reclaiming a Forgotten (and Essential) Small Group Experience*, by Kevin M. Watson. To order it or to read a sample chapter, visit http://store.seedbed.com/products/class-meeting-by-kevin -watson.

8. See Maxie D. Dunnam, *The Intercessory Life: A Missional Model for Discipleship*, available at http://store.seedbed.com/products/the-intercessory-life-breaking-the -impossibility-barrier-by-maxie-dunnam.

The Prayer

Lord Jesus, thank you for the truth of the gospel. Thank you for the way the truth of the gospel can be known personally in my own experience. And thank you for the way the truth of the gospel can move from my experience to original expressions of the gospel to other people. This is a mystery and a miracle. Come, Holy Spirit, and bring it all to bear in my life. In Jesus' name. Amen.

The Question

So how about it? Where are you strong in your faith—your understanding of the empirical/objective truth of Jesus; your experience of Jesus; your expression of Jesus in the world? Where are you weak? How might you grow in these ways?

34 Why the Opposite of Love Is Not Hate but Fear

1 JOHN 4:17–18 | This is how love is made complete among us so that we will have confidence on the day of judgment: In this world we are like Jesus. There is no fear in love. But perfect love drives out fear, because fear has to do with punishment. The one who fears is not made perfect in love.

Consider This

Over and over and over John brings us back to the hard objectivity of love over and against love as a soft, subjective sentiment. Humans are capable of all sorts of loving expressions. One minute we speak of how much we love that new restaurant across town, and the next of how much we love our spouses (and on Facebook, of all places).

We need a completely different way to categorize and talk about love when it comes to the way John employs the term, as well as how much of the rest of the New Testament does.

John chose the Greek term *agape* to capture what he meant by love. But still it begged the question. Sure, John could give a conceptual definition of *agape*—something like "the self-giving preferential treatment of another person at cost to yourself." I can grasp a definition like this, but I still don't know what it looks like. We insert the word *holy* in front of *love* to signify we are talking about love of another magnitude. The problem with all these definitions is the way they keep us talking around the subject. We must see an objective demonstration of this holy love of God. That's why John points to a person.

This is how love is made complete among us so that we will have confidence on the day of judgment: In this world we are like Jesus.

We must move beyond a conceptual definition of love to a boots-on-the-ground, love-looks-like-this (then fill in the blank) definition. Love looks like that time Jesus invited a despised tax collector to be his disciple. Love looks like that time Jesus struck up a conversation with the Samaritan woman of questionable reputation at the well. Love looks like that time Jesus saved his disciples' lives by speaking peace to a raging storm. Love looks like that time Jesus told a dead little girl's parents to not be afraid but to believe, after which he raised her back to life. Love looks like that time Jesus washed his disciples' feet.

There is no fear in love. But perfect love drives out fear, because fear has to do with punishment.

In each of these scenarios (and so many more), Jesus entered a situation characterized by fear and anxiety. Because his presence was the unadulterated expression of the holy love of God, fear and anxiety simply left. The presence of Jesus, which is to say the presence of holy love, drives out fear by displacing it.

The journey of becoming like Jesus can be described in many ways. In my judgment, chief among them would be the process from being a person of fear to becoming a person of love. So I ask you: What experience do you evoke in other people? Does your presence cause anxiety or unease or fear? Or does your presence exude a quality of peace that not only communicates that it is well with your soul, but that it is going to be OK for others too?

Remember: the path of following Jesus leads to perfect love; not because you will ever arrive at the place where you make no mistakes, but because the further we follow him, the more our presence exudes his presence. Jesus is himself the power of love in the face of fear. To the extent that you and I abide in Jesus, we become the power of love in the face of fear. To the extent that we don't, we are still part of the problem.

Are you ready to go to the next level? Remember: the opposite of love is not hate, but fear.

The Prayer

Lord Jesus, thank you for not only teaching about love, but for also showing us, time and time again, what real love looks like. Help us understand the difference between an ordinary act done in our own power and an ordinary act done in your power. I want to be done with fear so much so that I help others be done with fear too. I know the secret is more love, which means more of you. I pray in your name, Jesus. Amen.

The Question

Do you have a more anxious presence with others or a more peace-filled presence? How do you stay mindful of these realities?

35 We Hate because He First Hated Us

1 JOHN 4:19–21 | We love because he first loved us. Whoever claims to love God yet hates a brother or sister is a liar. For whoever does not love their brother and sister, whom they have seen, cannot love God, whom they have not seen. And he has given us this command: Anyone who loves God must also love their brother and sister.

Consider This

We love because he first loved us.

Sometimes, in order to break through last year's understanding, I will turn a verse upside down or over on its side to see if I can gain a fresh perspective. It's not so much that last year's understanding was wrong (though it may have been). The point is, last year's understanding may not be enough for this year's faith. As Paul wrote to the Corinthians, "Now we see in a mirror dimly" (1 Cor. 13:12 ESV).

So, does this mean the meaning of Scripture changes over time? Absolutely not. It deepens. The truth is the truth is the truth: yesterday, today, and forever. It does not depend on my perception, interpretation, or understanding. Love, however, is another matter. In order for my love to grow deeper in the ways of the love of God, my perception, interpretation, and understanding of the truth must deepen.

Back to flipping the text over, what if we put it this way: "We hate because he first hated us." In this instance, by "he," I refer to Satan, of course. Isn't that what's going on back in Eden in Genesis 3? It's a scene filled with misrepresentation, deception, and lying, the kind of things people do when they hate another person.

Jesus put it even stronger when he said, "The thief comes only to steal and kill and destroy; I have come that they may have life and have it to the full" (John 10:10). Satan hated humanity from day one to the present day. God, on the other hand, loved humanity from day one to the present day. Just as Scripture says, "We love because He first loved us," does it not follow that "we hate because he first hated us"? Is this not exactly what happened in Eden? If perfect love drives out fear, then fear, left to itself, will become hatred. And let's remember: hatred doesn't begin with our feelings. It begins with the small and often subtle ways we prefer ourselves at the expense of other people.

For instance, in the wake of Eden's fall, Adam and Eve hid themselves from each other. Because they broke their trust with God, their trust with one another was broken. This is what we do when we are afraid. Next, they hid from God. Once trust is broken, self-protection becomes the name of the game, and self-protection always comes at a cost to others. Remember what happened when God found them and inquired as to what had happened? Blame. Adam blamed Eve. Eve blamed Satan. Translation: everybody threw everybody else under the bus. That's how hatred does its best work, turning people against each other. Before you know it, they have a couple of kids out in the suburbs somewhere east of Eden, and one of the sons winds up murdering the other.

Let's go one more click in. Few of us would identify our big problem as hatred. The problem is anger. Anger thrives in a milieu of mistrust. Mistrust in our relationships feeds anger, and like a garden full of weeds, anger will literally suck the life out of it. From here it's a few short steps to contempt and hatred, and a couple more to retaliatory behavior, and only a few more to all-out war of either the hot or cold variety.

How about it? We hate because he first hated us. Unfortunately, this is the default position of the human race.

Without intervention, and whether we admit it or not, we inevitably contribute to the condition known as "on earth as it is in hell," and without intervention that's where we will all wind up.

Thank God there has been an intervention. It's called the gospel. I'll give it to you in seven words today: *we love because he first loved us.*

It's important we remember the gospel did not begin as God's response to sin. The gospel preceded sin. It even preceded creation. John said it yesterday: God is love, which is to say God is sacrificial, self-giving, overflowing, generous goodness—all the time. Before anything came to be, God— Father, Son, and Holy Spirit—dwelled together in the unapproachably holy love and light of the gospel.

We must come to grips with this fact: sin did not get the first word and it will not get the last. In creating the world, God first loved us. Original love preceded original sin. "He first loved us." When sin entered the scene and broke our trust relationship with God, he kept loving us. This is the intervention part.

"For God so loved the world that He gave His only begotten Son, that whosoever believeth in Him should not perish, but have everlasting life" (John 3:16 KJ21). We love because he first loved us.

"But God demonstrates his own love for us in this: While we were still sinners, Christ died for us" (Rom. 5:8).

OK, I've got to stop. But I want to make sure you are trusting Jesus. I want to know that you have crossed over from death to life and from hatred to love. I know: the vestiges of death and hatred still linger. We've got work to do on things like pride and anger—but we work from this place of knowing that "we love because he first loved us."

The Prayer

Lord Jesus, thank you for being the Lamb slain from the foundation of the world. I am grateful that your love is not a mere response to my sin. It's who you already were and ever shall be. Come, Holy Spirit, and ferret out my fear. Show it to me in my anger. Fill me with the overwhelming and overcoming love of God in Jesus Christ. It is in your name, Jesus, I pray. Amen.

The Question

How about your anger? What are you really angry about? What are you afraid of at the core of your being? How is that driving your life? How might this be arrested and subdued?

36 The Most Important Word in the Bible

1 JOHN 5:1–4 HCSB | Everyone who believes that Jesus is the Messiah has been born of God, and everyone who loves the Father also loves the one born of Him. This is how we know that we love God's children when we love God and obey

His commands. For this is what love for God is: to keep His commands. Now His commands are not a burden, because whatever has been born of God conquers the world. This is the victory that has conquered the world: our faith.

Consider This

What would you say is the most important word in today's reading? Would it be *Jesus* or *God* or *love* or *believes*, or how about *overcome*? Here's my vote: *everyone*. In fact, it may be the most important word in all of the Bible.

Everyone is such a powerful and beautiful word. It says you and me and all of us. No one has to be left out. It says there's more than enough room. Come one. Come all. This is the meaning of inclusive.

Everyone who believes. We aren't talking about intellectual assent here, but trusting faith. To believe means your life can be summed up in one word: *yes*.

Everyone who believes that Jesus is the Christ or Messiah. Most people who don't believe in Jesus don't refuse to believe because of Jesus but because of their displeasure in his followers. While this is understandable, it is not acceptable. Jesus stands on his own and in a category of his own, independent of his proponents or detractors. His words speak for themselves. His deeds tell their own story. His death on the cross stands as the signal day in the history of the human race, second only to his resurrection from the dead, which radiates the unquenchable, unstoppable truth of all the ages past and all eternity to come: everyone who believes Jesus is the Christ is born of God.

John says the same thing in a similar way in his gospel account:

> Yet to all who did receive him, to those who believed in his name, he gave the right to become children of God—children born not of natural descent, nor of human decision or a husband's will, but born of God. (John 1:12–13)

There's a final word to point out in today's text. Everyone who believes that Jesus is the Christ . . . *overcomes*.

This is not immunity to struggling or suffering or hardships or injustices or injury or pain or failures or anything else. The promise is to overcome.

Everyone. Who wouldn't take that offer? It is a very, very good deal. It is exceedingly good news.

Herein lies our mission. We want *everyone* to know about this offer, this very good deal, this exceedingly good news.

The Prayer

Lord Jesus, thank you for loving everyone and for giving everyone an opportunity to respond to your offer of grace. Make my life a winsome invitation to everyone I know or ever will know. In your name I pray, Jesus. Amen.

The Question

Have you responded to Jesus' offer of the life everlasting that begins now? Do you know people who have not responded? Do you know people who have no idea of the offer? What is a next step you might take toward these people?

Why Trouble Is Not a Problem

1 JOHN 5:5 | Who is it that overcomes the world? Only the one who believes that Jesus is the Son of God.

Consider This

The world is filled with trouble. From the trouble of tempt-ation to the trouble of tragedy, our lives are riddled with struggle and hardship. There are troubled marriages and troubled children. There's being in trouble with the law. Then there's that proverbial bridge over troubled waters. There's even a board game called Trouble.

The surprising thing is the way we seem to be continually surprised by the presence of trouble in our lives. So many people believe Jesus is their "Get Out of Jail Free" card. Ask the early Christians and they will tell you Jesus was more like a "Go Straight to Jail. Do Not Pass Go and Do Not Collect $200" card.

I once heard a preacher remark that there were only two kinds of people in the world: those who were facing trouble and those who were about to be facing trouble.

When you think about it, you realize the only real difference between rich people and poor people is the rich people can afford to hold their troubles at bay longer.

Jesus didn't mince words when it came to trouble. Here's how he put it near the end of his life. "I have told you these things, so that in me you may have peace. In this world you will have trouble. But take heart! I have overcome the world" (John 16:33).

Today's text makes it clear: there is no such thing as a trouble-free life. There is only the promise of overcoming.

Who is it that overcomes the world? Only the one who believes that Jesus is the Son of God.

To follow Jesus means to see trouble completely differently than the world sees trouble. We tend to have it exactly backward. We are surprised when we have trouble and doubtful that we can overcome it. Jesus says don't be surprised when you have trouble; just expect to overcome it. It's not a fatalistic or even pessimistic outlook on life, but it is a profound mind shift.

I remember being in a rural church in deep East Texas one night some years back. The song leader was leading the familiar old chorus "There's Something about That Name," by Bill and Gloria Gaither.

Right in the middle of the song, the worship leader suddenly stopped playing. He began telling a story as though he had just remembered it, of how his mother had taught him as a child that the simplest and most powerful prayer a person could say was simply the name *Jesus*—that his very name was a prayer.

Jesus. It's not a magic word, but it is the name above all names. It will only be at the sound of this name that every knee will bow and every tongue confess that Jesus Christ is Lord. On that day, not only will all the trouble in the world be over and done with, but it will all have been worth it.

Who is it that overcomes the world? Only the one who believes that Jesus is the Son of God.

The Prayer

Lord Jesus, thank you for telling us the truth about trouble. And thank you for your promise to be with us in the midst of trouble. Give me the faith and courage to follow you on the journey of overcoming. I pray in Jesus' name. Amen.

The Question

Do you tend to be the kind of person who is surprised by trouble and pessimistic about overcoming it? Are you becoming the kind of person who is not surprised by trouble but is filled with faith about overcoming it? How might you become more of this kind of person?

38 Ladies and Gentlemen of the Jury . . .

1 JOHN 5:6–8 ESV | This is he who came by water and blood—Jesus Christ; not by the water only but by the water and the blood. And the Spirit is the one who testifies, because the Spirit is the truth. For there are three that testify: the Spirit and the water and the blood; and these three agree.

Consider This

In my brief career as an attorney, nothing was more thrilling than to bring closing arguments at a trial and ask for a verdict.

That's exactly what John is up to here in the fifth and final chapter of his case. John has brought forth witness after witness in his masterful case against the false teachers and in support of the truth of the gospel.

In today's text, he's pulling it all together. He's rehearsing the case by reminding the jury (i.e., the young church) of the testimony from his star witnesses: the water and the blood and the Spirit.

False teachers attract a lot of followers, but each tends to be his or her own best witness. John is bringing not one or two but three authoritative witnesses to refute the witness of the false teachers.

So why does this matter to us now? Thanks for asking. It matters because every age has its own variety of false teachers. First John sounds the siren to steer clear of them. They sound plausible. They garner popularity. Rarely do they blatantly disregard the truth as much as they slightly shade it. It's these subtle shades of the truth that steer entire communities toward shipwreck. They can sound so reasonable; even impressive. They can sell thousands upon thousands of books.

Paul once wrote a letter to Timothy that sounded the same alarm. We will do well to rehearse it here:

> For the time will come when people will not put up with sound doctrine. Instead, to suit their own desires, they will gather around them a great number of teachers to say what their itching ears want to hear. They will turn their ears away from the truth and turn aside to myths. (2 Tim. 4:3–4)

Ladies and gentlemen of the jury, the time has come. People are not putting up with sound doctrine. False teaching abounds. We live in an age of itching ears. I join the apostle John in asking you for a verdict. Stand with the truth. Stand on the Word of God. Stand in the strength of the Holy Spirit. Never depart from the faith once handed down to the saints. No matter what. Church, we cannot abide a miscarriage of justice. We cannot afford a hung jury. Will you receive the testimony of these faithful witnesses?

What say you?

The Prayer

Lord Jesus, you are the bona fide, the authentic, the genuine article. Help us to become so familiar with you and your truth that we instantly recognize false teaching. Give us the discernment to recognize the first faint whisper of any teaching that departs from your truth, your ways, or your will. I follow you alone. I pray in your name, Jesus. Amen.

The Question

Can you think of any present-day scenarios where false teaching has damaged the faith of a person or a community? How did it happen? Are you familiar enough with Jesus and his teachings that you could recognize counterfeit teaching?

39 On Playing the God Card . . .

1 JOHN 5:9–10 | We accept human testimony, but God's testimony is greater because it is the testimony of God, which he has given about his Son. Whoever believes in the Son of God accepts this testimony. Whoever does not believe God has made him out to be a liar, because they have not believed the testimony God has given about his Son.

Consider This

It seems strange to put it this way, but in today's text, as John moves through his closing argument, he's making a move that requires extreme care. John plays the God card.

Sure, he's done it throughout his address in this sermonic letter, but he brings it hard here in the close. In making his case, John all at once has it much easier than we do, and yet much harder. It's easier because John is an eyewitness. All that John speaks of is recent history. People are still meeting at the empty tomb in Jerusalem. The world is being turned upside down by the gospel. It's harder because the New Testament was not the New Testament yet. John and others were writing what would later become the New Testament. Nobody's handing out Gideon's pocket New Testaments with the Psalms on the street corner. Sure, there are all sorts of credible human witnesses. Then again, these false teachers are also making a human witness to the contrary. While Paul writes 1 Corinthians, a host of other teachers are writing "2 Opinions."

It's why from the get-go John has been careful to say, "That which was from the beginning, which we have heard, which we have seen with our eyes, which we have looked at and our hands have touched—this we proclaim concerning the Word of life" (1 John 1:1).

This is why the Word of God matters so much. It was written by THE eyewitnesses. We aren't dealing with a "John told Paul to tell Timothy that Jesus was raised from the dead." In our New Testament, we have the direct evidence. The New

Testament we hold in our hands today is "God's testimony" as John phrases it in today's text.

Let me say it even plainer: the Word of God as witnessed in the Old and New Testaments of the Bible is God's testimony. Many people do not believe this. At them the mission of God is aimed. Unbelievers are not the problem. The problem is those who believe a distorted or errant version of the truth. When it comes to the bona fide Christian faith, people are not typically misled by unbelievers. They are misled by so-called Bible teachers who do not believe the whole truth and by self-styled Christian leaders who claim to treasure Scripture yet interpret the Scriptures to mean something they have never remotely meant before.

Here's the grave danger: false teachers will readily play the God card under the pretense that the Holy Spirit is revealing new truth and new doctrine, which effectively translates into a form of new Scripture, and they place it on the same level as the Old and New Testaments of the Bible as we know it. They claim that the writers of the New Testament were doing in their day the same thing that these new teachers are doing now: interpreting an ancient text according to the new revelation of the Holy Spirit. In other words, as the apostles were interpreting the Old Testament, these new "prophets" are now interpreting the New Testament. According to their hermeneutic (method of biblical interpretation), the Holy Spirit can reveal new truth that actually contradicts Scripture. Do you see the problem with this? History is littered with these kinds of teachers. In their wake follow wave on wave of well-meaning people shipwrecked in their faith on the shoals of heresies and half-truths, bailing water from their boats with broken buckets.

Here's what I would like to say about that. It is human testimony. It is not God's testimony. Be very careful when people start playing the God card in ways that contravene God's testimony as we have it in the Bible. In fact, because of the Holy Spirit–inspired way John and the other writers of the New Testament so judiciously played the God card, we don't have to. We can simply stand on the testimony, and stand we must—not with our gospel guns raised to shoot, but as humble lovers of the truth, ready to quietly serve or boldly speak up as the calling of faith requires.

False teachers can be fairly called enemies of the gospel, yet Jesus demands that we love them with holy love. He just won't let us give them a pass. It's about speaking the truth in love. Paul put it well when he wrote to the Ephesian church, also in the throes of false teachers, to grow into maturity, even the whole measure of the fullness of Christ:

> Then we will no longer be little children, tossed by the waves and blown around by every wind of teaching, by human cunning with cleverness in the techniques of deceit. But speaking the truth in love, let us grow in every way into Him who is the head—Christ. (Eph. 4:14–15 HCSB)

The Prayer

Lord Jesus, thank you for being the same, yesterday, today, and forever. And I am thankful that your teaching is also the same yesterday, today, and forever. Rather than bending your teaching to fit my understanding, let me bend my understanding to align with your teaching. Come, Holy Spirit, and lead me into mature faith. I pray in your name, Jesus. Amen.

The Question

Do you think the Holy Spirit is still revealing new truths that carry the same authority as the Scripture? How can we gently rebuke anything that contradicts or contravenes the Word of God while courageously standing on the unshakable truth of the gospel?

40 Why We've Gotten Eternal Life Wrong

1 JOHN 5:11–12 | And this is the testimony: God has given us eternal life, and this life is in his Son. Whoever has the Son has life; whoever does not have the Son of God does not have life.

Consider This

Eternal life. What is the meaning of eternal life? Somewhere along the way, eternal became primarily understood as quantitative. It became another way of meaning infinite, or higher than one can count. In other words, we think about eternal life in the same way that we think about time.

The highly popular last verse of "Amazing Grace," which, incidentally, was added to the hymn years after it was composed, makes the point:

> When we've been there ten thousand years
> Bright shining as the sun
> We've no less days to sing God's praise
> Than when we'd first begun.

See what I mean? We think of eternal life in terms of years and days, which naturally is the only category we can really grasp. Here's the big problem with this way of thinking. It tends to create an unfortunate and very limited category for eternal life. If we think of it as an extension of time, we will primarily consider it as something that happens after time as we know it ends. There's life and death and eternal life. Eternal life must mean the extension of our life beyond our death.

At this point I want both to assure you that eternal life at the very least means the extension of our life beyond our death, and to stretch your understanding to a much larger and more biblical way of grasping it. This is going to sound deep, but stick with me. It's important. Time and eternity are two separate yet coexisting realities. Time is not a feature of eternity. The big miracle is that because of Jesus, eternity has made itself a feature of time. (I know: deep thought. But you're smart. Hang with me.)

The Bible reveals a bigger picture. It gives us life in three basic epochs: first, the creation. Second, the fall from grace, which inaugurated "the present evil age" (Gal. 1:4). And third, "the age to come" (Matt. 12:32; Mark 10:30 et al.). Here's the kicker. The age to come was inaugurated with the coming of Jesus Christ. He was and is the eternal life. Think back through his life on earth and all the ways he reversed the agendas of sin and death. Jesus' life was one massive take-down of death—right up to the present day. In fact, remember the very opening of 1 John with me:

> The life appeared; we have seen it and testify to it, and we proclaim to you the eternal life, which was with the Father and has appeared to us. (1:2)

You see, death is not something that happens to us when we die. It's something we carry around in our bodies that finally takes us down. Death is the disease we are born with and the one that will eventually kill us. It's why the great quest of all of human history, from the search for the fountain of youth to time travel to the revolutionary new juice diets, has been to find a cure for death. The best we've been able to manage is to extend our life expectancy by a few decades. Why all this? Because in the deepest place of our soul, we remember Eden. We know that we know that we know we are not created for death. We are created for life, and not just endless life but eternal life.

In the midst of this present evil age, death seems to win. This is why the resurrection from the dead was such a long-anticipated sign for God's people. The resurrection from the dead would signify the defeat of death and the beginning of the age to come. The age to come is nothing short of the kingdom of God on earth as it is in heaven. With the death, resurrection, and ascension of Jesus and the sending of the Holy Spirit, the age to come has actually broken in on the present evil age.

And this is the testimony: God has given us eternal life, and this life is in his Son. Whoever has the Son has life; whoever does not have the Son of God does not have life.

Eternal life is not that portion of life that begins after we die. No, eternal life is the person of Jesus Christ. Eternal life means the restoration of human beings to God's original intentions—in other words, like Jesus Christ. Eternal life is a qualitative change, one dimension of which is the end of thinking about time as a quantitative reality. Eternal life is the infusion of the very life of God into a human person. It has a durable nature of an unending quality. It's why one of the church's most ancient songs says, "As it was in the beginning, is now, and ever shall be, world without end. Amen. Amen."[9]

BEFORE: We have primarily thought of eternal life as a conceptual albeit real truth meant to comfort us concerning the shortness of our life on earth and the promise of something much better later. The general sentiment is, "You are going to die, but don't worry. You will live forever if you believe in Jesus."

---

9. "Glory Be to the Father," a.k.a. "Gloria Patri."

NOW: We must grasp eternal life as the intervention of Jesus Christ into the present evil age to inaugurate the age to come right in the midst of it—something akin to a table in the presence of our enemies. When he returns to the earth, there will be the final cataclysmic consummation of his kingdom, but it is now a very real and powerful, growing concern. The promise is every bit as present tense as it is future tense. It is the right-now infusion of eternal life—which is to say, the life of God—into human beings to remake them together into a people whose presence manifests the presence of God, the overwhelming power of holy love in which nothing is impossible.

According to our text today, this life is given exclusively in Jesus Christ, the second person of the Trinity, the Son of God, and extended inclusively to all who will believe and receive it. That's the gospel.

Folks, we won't be there ten thousand years, as the song goes—because no one will be counting!

The Prayer

Lord Jesus, you are eternal life and to know you is to know eternal life. Help me grasp the truth that eternal life cannot be measured in days and years, that is not something that happens after death. Come, Holy Spirit, and lead me into the reality of eternal life now. I pray in your name, Jesus. Amen.

The Question

Have you primarily thought of eternal life as something you will have after death? Where do you wrestle with today's teaching about eternal life? Are you ready to welcome and walk in eternal life today? What might that mean for you?

41 Why Discipleship Is Not Preparation for Eternal Life

1 JOHN 5:13–15 | I write these things to you who believe in the name of the Son of God so that you may know that you have eternal life. This is the confidence we have in approaching God: that if we ask anything according to his will, he hears us. And if we know that he hears us—whatever we ask—we know that we have what we asked of him.

Consider This

John continues his march toward a verdict. Yesterday his closing argument turned toward the *big point* of the whole letter. He has taken on the false teachers so strongly because they were steering the young church away from the *main thing*. In the end, this is not a prosecution of the false teachers but a proclamation of the gospel of Jesus Christ.

So what's the *big point* and the *main thing*? Thanks for asking. It's *eternal life*. The gospel is all about eternal life. As I wrote yesterday, I don't think I've really understood eternal life.

In one of Jesus' nine recorded prayers, the longest one known as his high priestly prayer (see John 17), Jesus prays as follows: "Now this is eternal life: that they know you, the only true God, and Jesus Christ, whom you have sent" (John 17:3).

We talk about the gospel as salvation from sin, justification, sanctification, deliverance from death, the abundant life, becoming a new creation, and to be sure, it is all these things. All of these things can be summarized in the two words *eternal life*.

John wants those who have believed in Jesus to understand the new truth about themselves: "I write these things to you who believe in the name of the Son of God so that you may know that you have eternal life" (1 John 5:13). Note where he goes next.

> This is the confidence we have in approaching God: that if we ask anything according to his will, he hears us. And if we know that he hears us—whatever we ask—we know that we have what we asked of him. (vv. 14–15)

Note he's talking about eternal life in the framework of discipleship—in this instance—prayer. Eternal life is not in the category of funeral preparations and what happens after one dies. Eternal life is the whole tamale. In fact, I'm beginning to think of discipleship in a new way. Discipleship is nothing more or less than the retrofitting of a human being with the gift of eternal life. Eternal life was lost as a consequence of the fall from grace. It is now gained as the gift of God, given to those who place their faith in Jesus Christ. Discipleship is the process of learning to express in reality what has in fact become real and true. Discipleship is not preparation for eternal life; it's practicing eternal life.

What if this is the organizing principle or the governing dynamic of all of life—eternal life? We need to *know* we possess eternal life, and then we need to be trained in how to fully live into eternal life. Because we have largely thought of eternal life as what happens when we die, we have never really gotten around to living into it before our death. This helps make sense of all of the New Testament teaching on dying before you die. Here's a representative example.

> Now if Christ is in you, the body is dead because of sin, but the Spirit is life because of righteousness. And if the Spirit of Him who raised Jesus from the dead lives in you, then He who raised Christ from the dead will also bring your mortal bodies to life through His Spirit who lives in you.
>
> So then, brothers [and sisters], we are not obligated to the flesh to live according to the flesh, for if you live according to the flesh, you are going to die. But if by the Spirit you put to death the deeds of the body, you will live. (Rom. 8:10–13 HCSB)

Now take a look at Romans 8 and examine it through the lens of eternal life.

Engaging with Scripture, prayer, fasting, encouraging one another in faith, and receiving the Lord's Supper all become the ways and means of nourishing the eternal life within us. Living generously, serving extravagantly, and loving boldly become the ways and means of nourishing the eternal life among us.

Eternal life . . . it's all about the extraordinary life of God indwelling and illuminating the lives of ordinary people.

The Prayer

Lord Jesus, you are the Eternal Life and to know you is to experience eternal life. In thinking this is something that we gain only after our death, we have missed it in our life. Turn that around in us today. Open the eyes of our hearts to see and hear and experience what we have known but not understood. Come, Holy Spirit, and make us truly alive with the Life that is life. I pray in your name, Jesus. Amen.

The Question

Do you know that you have eternal life? Are you experiencing eternal life now? How might you take the next step in appropriating this reality in your real life? What is keeping you from it?

12 Getting on with the Gospel

1 JOHN 5:16–17 | If you see any brother or sister commit a sin that does not lead to death, you should pray and God will give them life. I refer to those whose sin does not lead to death. There is a sin that leads to death. I am not saying that you should pray about that. All wrongdoing is sin, and there is sin that does not lead to death.

Consider This

Today's text is difficult to understand.

It's very hard to understand the particular context John is speaking into and the problem he is addressing when he says to not pray for people who are committing sin that leads to death.

John has named three sins that lead to death: disbelief in Jesus Christ, disobeying God's commands, and not loving brothers and sisters. He is basically speaking of people who are walking in the dark.

According to the tenor of the New Testament, we must pray for people who are proceeding down a path that leads to death.

What I find most interesting about today's text is this idea that if we pray for brothers and sisters who are caught in some kind of sin—that doesn't lead to death—the result is God will give them life.

The bigger and, in this instance, more implicit implication is the incompatibility of eternal life with sin and death. As we come to the end of John's message, we need to be reminded of one of the major assumptions of the New Testament: eternal life means freedom from sin and ultimate deliverance from death. Sin has lost its power, and death has lost its sting. The New Testament repeatedly calls us to live into the new reality of eternal life. Here's another example.

> So, you too consider yourselves dead to sin but alive to God in Christ Jesus. (Rom. 6:11 HCSB)

Today's text might be practically summarized as follows: "It's time to get on with the gospel, to receive the gift of the Holy Spirit and to claim the promise of eternal life, and we must pray for, encourage, and help one another to do the same." That's exactly what I'm trying to do with the daily text day after day after day—to help us get on with the gospel, receive the gift of the Holy Spirit, and live into the promise of eternal life.

It does not advance by amping up our commitment. It happens through becoming gut-level honest with ourselves (and each other) about our own desires. We must keep asking ourselves the hard questions, like . . .

Do I really desire to get on with the gospel?

Do I desire to be continually filled with the Holy Spirit?

Did I desire to live into the promise of eternal life today? How about tomorrow?

How about now?

The Prayer

Lord Jesus, you are eternal life and to know you is to experience eternal life now. Reveal to me the plain truth that my lack of experience of eternal life is actually a revelation of the quality of my relationship with you. Come, Holy Spirit, and grow my relationship with Jesus, in ways I can't even imagine now. I pray in your name, Jesus. Amen.

The Question

Why do people settle for and even substitute religious practice instead of pressing into a deeper relationship with Jesus Christ? Do you really want to grow beyond your own level of relationship with Jesus? What will this mean? How might you welcome this more boldly into your life? Are you so dissatisfied with the status quo that you will take a risk of going for it in a way you have not before?

43 Could the New Testament Be Wrong?

1 JOHN 5:18–20 | We know that anyone born of God does not continue to sin; the One who was born of God keeps them safe, and the evil one cannot harm them. We know that we are children of God, and that the whole world is under the control of the evil one. We know also that the Son of God has come and has given us understanding, so that we may know him who is

true. And we are in him who is true by being in his Son Jesus Christ. He is the true God and eternal life.

Consider This

In the May 20 entry of Oswald Chambers's *My Utmost for His Highest*, he wrote,

> Many of us prefer to stay at the threshold of the Christian life instead of going on to construct a soul in accordance with the new life God has put within. We fail because we are ignorant of the way we are made, we put things down to the devil instead of our own undisciplined natures. Think what we can be when we are roused!

It's taken me more than a hundred pages to say what Chambers said in a short paragraph. The New Testament teaches us what it means to "construct a soul in accordance with the new life God has put within." This captures the very essence of discipleship—as noted earlier—the retrofitting of a human being with eternal life.

We know that anyone born of God does not continue to sin; the One who was born of God keeps them safe, and the evil one cannot harm them.

"We fail because we are ignorant of the way we are made."

IMHO (in my humble opinion), the people of God are arrested in development; as Chambers put it, stuck at the "threshold of the Christian life," between the first half of the gospel and the second half.

It comes down to one of two possibilities: (1) either the New Testament is wrong, or (2) we aren't getting it.

Which possibility are you landing on?

The Prayer

Lord Jesus, thank you for not giving up on us. Thank you for your patience with us as we have thought we were in the house only to find we have been lingering at the door. I'm ready to move on from milk to meat, from my own meager and measured religion to mature faith. Come, Holy Spirit, and take me by the hand and lead me. I pray in your name, Jesus. Amen.

The Question

Are you ready to take significant next steps in the work of constructing a soul "in accordance with the new life God has put within"? Could it be that your going it alone is what is holding you back? How might you welcome another person or two to join you in this journey into the second half of the gospel?

Why the Last Words May Be the Most Important Words

1 JOHN 5:21 | Dear children, keep yourselves from idols.

Consider This

Wow! What a surprise ending. It's unforgettable. John didn't give any farewells or good wishes or "thanks for reading" or "let me summarize my three points" or a nice, tear-jerking antidote or anything of the sort.

He just stopped. John hasn't so much as whispered the word "idol" in anything he's written: not the gospel or 2 or 3 John. It's unprecedented for him.

Truth be told, I can only remember the way one other book in the New Testament ends. That would be the gospel of Matthew:

> "Therefore go and make disciples of all nations, baptizing them in the name of the Father and of the Son and of the Holy Spirit, and teaching them to obey everything I have commanded you. And surely I am with you always, to the very end of the age." (28:19–20)

"Keep yourselves from idols." So what's an idol? It's a substitute god. It's whatever promises to make your life work in exchange for your pursuit of it. Money comes to mind. It's why Jesus said so much about it—like, for instance, you can't serve God and money (see Matthew 6:24).

Honestly, I kind of want to wrap 1 John all up and tie a bow around it. If I'm true to John, I can't do it.

If you want people to remember the last thing you say, don't say something predictable. Don't even try to say something memorable. Just make your point and stop talking.

So how about this for an ending: *Dear children, keep yourselves from idols.*

Or how about I end by telling you the only possible way to actually keep yourselves from idols.

Entrust your life completely, constantly, and unreservedly to Jesus.

The Prayer

Lord Jesus, I entrust myself completely, constantly, and unreservedly to you. Yes, Lord, I do. Lead me now into the reality of this entrustment. By the power of your Spirit, I will keep myself from idols. I pray in your name, Jesus. Amen.

The Question

What keeps you from completely, constantly, and unreservedly entrusting yourself to Jesus? What are you afraid this might mean for you? Is it worth it to keep holding back? How might you actualize this movement in your life today? Tomorrow? The day after that?

The Sower's Creed

Today,
I sow for a great awakening.

Today,
I stake everything on the promise of the Word of God. I depend entirely on the power of the Holy Spirit. I have the same mind in me that was in Christ Jesus. Because Jesus is good news and Jesus is in me, I am good news.

Today,
I will sow the extravagance of the gospel everywhere I go and into everyone I meet.

Today,
I will love others as Jesus has loved me.

Today,
I will remember that the tiniest seeds become the tallest trees; that the seeds of today become the shade of tomorrow; that the faith of right now becomes the future of the everlasting kingdom.

Today,
I sow for a great awakening.